New Directions for
Student Services

John H. Schuh
EDITOR-IN-CHIEF

Elizabeth J. Whitt
ASSOCIATE EDITOR

Assisting Bereaved College Students

Heather L. Servaty-Seib
Deborah J. Taub
EDITORS

Number 121 • Spring 2008
Jossey-Bass
San Francisco

ASSISTING BEREAVED COLLEGE STUDENTS
Heather L. Servaty-Seib, Deborah J. Taub (eds.)
New Directions for Student Services, no. 121
John H. Schuh, Editor-in-Chief
Elizabeth J. Whitt, Associate Editor

NEW DIRECTIONS FOR STUDENT SERVICES (ISSN 0164-7970, e-ISSN 1536-0695) is part of The Jossey-Bass Higher and Adult Education Series and is published quarterly by Wiley Subscription Services, Inc., A Wiley Company, at Jossey-Bass, 989 Market Street, San Francisco, California 94103-1741. Periodicals Postage Paid at San Francisco, California, and at additional mailing offices. POSTMASTER: Send address changes to New Directions for Student Services, Jossey-Bass, 989 Market Street, San Francisco, CA 94103-1741.

New Directions for Student Services is indexed in CIJE: Current Index to Journals in Education (ERIC), Contents Pages in Education (T&F), Current Abstracts (EBSCO), Education Index/Abstracts (H.W. Wilson), Educational Research Abstracts Online (T&F), ERIC Database (Education Resources Information Center), and Higher Education Abstracts (Claremont Graduate University).

Microfilm copies of issues and articles are available in 16mm and 35mm, as well as microfiche in 105mm, through University Microfilms Inc., 300 North Zeeb Road, Ann Arbor, Michigan 48106-1346.

SUBSCRIPTIONS cost $85 for individuals and $209 for institutions, agencies, and libraries in the United States. See ordering information page at end of book.

EDITORIAL CORRESPONDENCE should be sent to the Editor-in-Chief, John H. Schuh, N 243 Lagomarcino Hall, Iowa State University, Ames, Iowa 50011.

www.josseybass.com

Contents

EDITORS' NOTES

Bereavement is a life transition or crisis faced by a significant number of undergraduates. Researchers have found that at any one point in time, approximately 25 percent of college students are in the first year of bereavement and almost 50 percent have experienced the death of a family member or friend within the past two years (Balk, 2001; Hardison, Neimeyer, and Lichstein, 2005). Death loss experiences and grief reactions have the potential to affect the day-to-day functioning and overall development of bereaved college students.

In addition, campuses experience the deaths of members of their student body. The mortality rate for individuals between the ages of eighteen and twenty-four, when combined for both sexes and all races, is about 1 per 1,000 (Anderson and Smith, 2005). The rates are even higher for the older age groups that comprise the adult learner population (Minino and others, 2007). Despite the prevalence and significance of death issues on campus, the topics of death, grief, and bereavement are seldom addressed in the student services literature.

Coping with Death on Campus, edited by Ellen Zinner, was published in the New Directions for Student Services series in 1985. It was a landmark contribution because it focused on college students as a unique group of grievers and provided practical guidance to student affairs professionals. The volume continues to be cited by researchers in the fields of higher education and thanatology (the study of death and dying), but it is now out of print.

What's more, the Zinner volume is more than twenty years old. In the intervening years, considerable theoretical, empirical, and clinical literature on death and dying has been produced. Although much of that literature has implications for work with college students, it has not been compiled and applied to them systematically.

Our goal in creating this sourcebook was to bring together perspectives from the fields of higher education and thanatology and to provide a mix of theoretical, research, and practice perspectives for coping with death and bereavement on campus. Of course, institutions have unique characteristics, and the composition of student populations differs widely. The materials and guidelines presented in this book should therefore be considered in light of these contextual factors.

Chapters One, Two, and Three set the stage for a consideration of bereavement among college students. In Chapter One, David E. Balk discusses the implications of the consistent findings that between 22 and 30 percent of undergraduates are in the first year of grieving the death of a family member

NEW DIRECTIONS FOR STUDENT SERVICES, no. 121, Spring 2008   © Wiley Periodicals, Inc.
Published online in Wiley InterScience (www.interscience.wiley.com) • DOI: 10.1002/ss.261

or a friend. In Chapter Two, Deborah J. Taub and Heather L. Servaty-Seib use student development theory as a lens through which to consider the ways in which students cope with death. Although many student development theories focus primarily on traditional-age students, the authors have indicated where their insights might be applied to older students. In Chapter Three, Robert A. Neimeyer and his colleagues bring together the findings of several studies on how bereaved college students make meaning in the face of loss and offer guidance for assisting bereaved students.

Chapters Four and Five focus on the use of workshops and training to provide both direct and indirect support to bereaved students. In Chapter Four, Craig J. Vickio presents information and guidelines for grief workshops for bereaved students. In Chapter Five, Heather L. Servaty-Seib and Deborah J. Taub describe how two groups in the campus community who have frequent contact with students—faculty members and resident assistants—can be trained in ways to understand and support grieving students.

Chapters Six, Seven, and Eight shift attention to administrative responses to death. In Chapter Six, Heidi Levine examines the dynamics of emotional responses to death by suicide in the campus community as well as beneficial ways for campuses to respond after a suicide. Lou Ann Hamilton, in Chapter Seven, draws from her experiences at Purdue University to provide guidelines for death notification. Finally, in Chapter Eight, Cheryl M. Callahan and Erin K. Fox give practical guidance regarding a broad range of considerations in the aftermath of a student death.

Death is a fact of life for college students, whether they are traditional-age or adult learners, undergraduates or graduate students, full-time or part-time students, or on-campus residents or commuters. Members of the higher education community need to be ready to respond with support and assistance when death touches the lives of students. We hope that this sourcebook provides useful guidance for a caring response.

Heather L. Servaty-Seib
Deborah J. Taub
Editors

References

Anderson, R. N., and Smith, B. S. "Deaths: Leading Causes for 2002." *National Vital Statistics Reports,* 2005, *53,* no. 17.
Balk, D. E. "College Student Bereavement, Scholarship, and the University: A Call for University Engagement." *Death Studies,* 2001, *25,* 67–84.
Hardison, H. G., Neimeyer, R. A., and Lichstein, K. L. "Insomnia and Complicated Grief Symptoms in Bereaved College Students." *Behavioral Sleep Medicine,* 2005, *3,* 99–111.
Minino, A. M., Heron, M. P., Murphy, S. L., and Kochanek, M. A. "Deaths: Final for 2004." *National Vital Statistics Reports,* 2007, *55,* no. 19.
Zinner, E. S. (ed.). *Coping with Death on Campus.* New Directions for Student Services, no. 31. San Francisco: Jossey-Bass, 1985.

HEATHER L. SERVATY-SEIB *is associate professor of educational studies at Purdue University, first vice-president of the Association for Death Education, and a counseling psychologist in private practice.*

DEBORAH J. TAUB *is associate professor of higher education and coordinator of the graduate program in higher education at the University of North Carolina at Greensboro.*

1

*The author offers evidence that 22 to 30 percent of college
undergraduates are in the first year of bereavement,
reviews the effects of their grieving, and addresses implications for colleges and universities.*

Grieving: 22 to 30 Percent of All College Students

David E. Balk

At any given time, 22 to 30 percent of college undergraduates are in the first
twelve months of grieving the death of a family member or friend. This conclusion, startling to some but accepted by others, comes from a variety of
sources at academic sites in the United States and Europe. Information
about the prevalence rate resulted from clinical observations and anecdotal
reflections and from empirical studies using convenience samples. No carefully designed study using random sampling has examined bereavement's
prevalence among college students, but conviction that the 22 to 30 percent
figure is correct is growing. Some researchers have begun examining the
effects of college student bereavements, effects that unfold as bereavement
extends from the first twelve months.

In this chapter, I examine the formal and informal bases for beliefs in
the 22 to 30 percent prevalence rate and consider what empirical studies
have uncovered about manifestations of bereavement in the lives of college
students. I conclude by posing the question "What relevance, if any, does
this information have for universities and colleges?" and offer some initial
answers.

Data Sources for Prevalence Assertions

Anecdotal Evidence. In the late 1980s and early 1990s, most college
administrators and faculty members I knew expressed skepticism that 22 to
30 percent of college undergraduates were in the first year of bereavement.

NEW DIRECTIONS FOR STUDENT SERVICES, no. 121, Spring 2008   © Wiley Periodicals, Inc.
Published online in Wiley InterScience (www.interscience.wiley.com) • DOI: 10.1002/ss.262

They considered the survey findings (officially reported in Balk, 1997, but informally discussed from the early 1990s) a fluke and, because the findings came from convenience rather than random sampling, doubted that the 22 to 30 percent assertion offered a true picture. Then, one day in 1993 in conversation with the president of Kansas State University, I mentioned my interest in college student bereavement and asked, "President Wefald, what percentage of undergraduates do you think are in the first year of bereavement?" He responded, without hesitation, "Oh, about 25 percent." When in astonishment I confirmed this estimate and asked how he knew, he simply stated, "David, I've been intimately connected with higher education and college students for too many years not to know." Since that conversation, a few other college administrators have indicated that it does not surprise them that empirical studies have uncovered a 22 to 30 percent prevalence rate. It has become clear to me, however, that many persons' responses to learning there is such a high proportion of bereaved students is "So what?" These persons have experienced bereavement themselves, know that they worked through it, and consider it a human misfortune for which people do not need professional care. In this reaction, they agree with Freud ([1917] 1957), who maintained that normal bereavement is not a pathological disturbance requiring professional intervention.

Clinical Observation. Counselors and other mental health professionals at college counseling centers have remarked that issues of loss affect a significant percentage of the students who come to them for help. These counselors worked at four universities where I have taught: Kansas State University, Oklahoma State University, City University of New York at Brooklyn College, and the University of Arizona. Students did not see, however, that issues of loss were problems to bring to a counselor's attention. Loss, often unresolved, simply formed the story of the students' lives, and knowledge of the loss came out as the skilled helpers allowed the students to tell their stories. Counselors at all these institutions expressed confidence that bereavement was a defining issue in the lives of no less than 40 percent of the students on the campus but was not a matter needing professional help. They believed that only a small proportion of students, somehow stuck in their grief, would benefit from counseling.

Empirical Study. Mortality rates on college campuses provide one source of data from which to infer the prevalence of bereavement among college students. Wrenn (1991) noted that annual rates of death of students ranged from 4 to 15 per 10,000 students, and extrapolating from the total student population in the United States, he inferred that anywhere from 5,000 to 18,750 students die each year. Most of these deaths are due to vehicular accidents, but there is alarm over the rising incidence of college student suicides (Haas, 2004): 7.5 suicides for every 100,000 college students. Alcohol is thought to have a role in many of these deaths (Hingson and others, 2002), and alcohol-related deaths are likely to continue as a result of binge drinking among college students (Hingson, Heeren, Winter, and Wechsler, 2005).

In addition to the family members who grieve the death of a college student, the lives of students who knew the deceased are likely to be affected; in cases of student deaths due to driving under the influence, approximately one million students might also be left with physical injuries (Hingson, Heeren, Winter, and Wechsler, 2005). Effects of deaths of students on others thus account for part of the 22 to 30 percent bereavement prevalence rate.

LaGrand (1985, 1986) was the first to publish comprehensive empirical data on college student bereavement. He conducted a survey of college students in the state of New York and identified a variety of losses in many of their lives, among them the deaths of family members and friends. The deaths of loved ones accounted for nearly 30 percent of all the losses reported. LaGrand (1986) asserted that the public in general and the college community in particular dismiss the serious and continuing impacts that unresolved bereavement impose on young adults.

A study done over five semesters (1988 to 1991) at Kansas State University produced further empirical support that college student bereavement is more widespread than many persons had realized (Balk, 1997). Students enrolled in a human development course were invited to participate in a survey that included questions about bereavement; 994 students (68.8 percent of those enrolled) agreed to participate in the survey.

Most of the students (81.8 percent) indicated that a family death (most were of grandparents or great-grandparents) had occurred. Nearly 20 percent reported multiple family deaths. For example, one twenty-two-year-old undergraduate reported that her father, sister, brother, and grandparent had all died. Although the average time since a family member's death was 4.4 years, 29.4 percent of participants reported that a family member had died within the previous twelve months, and 47.2 percent said one or more family members had died within the previous twenty-four months. Most of the deaths (83 percent) had been due to illness.

About three-fifths of the survey respondents (59.8 percent) indicated that a friend had died, and many of these students (46.6 percent) said they had been close or very close to the person who had died. On average, it had been 2.5 years since the friend's death, and 27 percent of the students surveyed (268 of the 994 respondents) said the death had been within the past twelve months. Over 38 percent (549 students) said that a friend had died within the past twenty-four months. Most of the deaths (62.4 percent) had been due to vehicular accidents, 18 percent to illness (primarily cancer), 11.3 percent to suicide, and 6.2 percent to homicide.

Eighteen students in the survey volunteered to participate in an in-depth follow-up interview. Most of these students were in the first year of bereavement following the death of a family member or of a friend. All of the students acknowledged that students unaffected by the death underestimated the intensity and duration of their grief reactions; they also reported that prior to their own bereavement, they would not have thought grief could be so intense or last so long.

This study's limitations—it was conducted at one midwestern land grant university; used cross-sectional, convenience sampling techniques; included few in-depth follow-up interviews; and had an ethnically homogeneous sample (94 percent white)—have not deterred faculty and counselors at other universities from acknowledging that the findings about the prevalence of student bereavement mirror their experiences.

Manifestations of Bereavement in the Lives of College Students

Scholarly examination of college student bereavement has been scanty but is increasing. To this small body of literature we can add information gathered from clinical and other interventions with bereaved students. Most of what we know about the phenomenon of college student bereavement is framed in terms of psychological reactions. We know that the cascading effects of bereavement present difficulties for eighteen- to twenty-three-year-old college students and enduring obstacles for those whose mourning is complicated. We know some bereaved students seek help at student mental health centers, but the overall ratio of student enrollment at the university to caseloads at counseling centers indicates that seeking help is the exception rather than the rule.

A holistic template about bereavement's effects describes the multifaceted impacts that irreparable loss can have in the life of the grieving student. This holistic template identifies six areas affected by grief: the physical, behavioral, interpersonal, cognitive, emotional, and spiritual. This template is formed from frameworks including Lindemann's acute grief syndrome (1944), Attig's existential phenomenological analysis of grief (1996), Bowlby's use of attachment theory (1980), the emerging import given to meaning-making (Jordan and Neimeyer, 2003; Neimeyer, Prigerson, and Davies, 2002), and the surge of attention toward continuing bonds in the life of the bereaved (Klass, Silverman, and Nickman, 1996).

Physical Effects of Bereavement. Bereavement often has physical effects on college students (Balk and Vesta, 1998; Hardison, Neimeyer, and Lichstein, 2005; King, 1998; Oltjenbruns, 1996). One of these involves sleep problems.

Insomnia has been identified as a significant somatic symptom of college students in the first and second year of bereavement; insomnia has been found to be particularly characteristic of the experience of college students with higher scores on a standardized inventory measuring complicated grief (Hardison, Neimeyer, and Lichstein, 2005). It is not surprising that bereaved college students, exhausted from lack of sleep, talk about how much effort and energy were required for what used to be normal activities such as climbing three flights of stairs to a classroom (see Balk and Vesta, 1998).

Behavioral Effects of Bereavement. Lindemann (1944) noted that a major behavioral effect of bereavement is loss of patterns of conduct. In line with this finding, bereaved college students have difficulty staying organized, managing their time, and meeting deadlines (Balk, Tyson-Rawson, and Colletti-Wetzel, 1993; Balk and Vesta, 1998). Some bereaved students engage in religious practices, such as praying and reading scriptures, behavior that could be seen to spill over into interpersonal aspects (Bible study and prayer with others) and cognitive effects (searching for meaning via religious frameworks) (Park, 2005).

Interpersonal Effects of Bereavement. What is known about effects of bereavement on college students' interpersonal relationships? Unanticipated negative outcomes of bereavement for college students include secondary losses and incremental grief as unaffected friends dismiss the intensity and duration of grief, find a person's ongoing grief both disquieting and wearisome, and shun the griever (Balk and Vesta, 1998; Oltjenbruns, 1996).

Cognitive Effects of Bereavement. Problems concentrating, studying, and remembering, with subsequent effects on grades and even college persistence, are the most obvious manifestations of cognitive effects of bereavement in the lives of college students (Balk, 2001; Balk and Vesta, 1998). Servaty-Seib and Hamilton (2006) noted that bereaved students' grades dropped significantly in the first semester of bereavement. Given the immediacy of the impact of poor grades on the bereaved student and given the impact of poor academic performance on student completion of degree programs and pursuit of professional careers, timely institutional responses to meet these academic needs seem warranted and consistent with the university's mission to facilitate student development.

Emotional Effects of Bereavement. An anecdote from a twenty-year-old woman whose fiancé had died vividly illustrates the emotional effects. One evening a few weeks after her fiancé's death in a high-speed car crash, Karen was sitting on her bed and burst suddenly and violently into tears. She didn't want to be crying but couldn't stop herself and gasped for breath as she sobbed and wept. The intensity and duration of this first crying spell frightened her, and similar spells occurred numerous times thereafter. As with nearly all bereaved college students I have met, Karen reported that her friends did not appreciate how intensely painful her emotional reactions were and did not understand why these reactions continued for months following her loss.

Spiritual Effects of Bereavement. People suffering the spiritual effects of bereavement are looking for answers to the existential question "Why?" This questioning reveals that the bereaved person is reassessing assumptions about reality. Questions about goodness, purpose, fairness, and meaning emerge, as well as questions about interrelatedness and isolation (see Attig, 1996).

Clinical Interventions and Other Responses. Loss occurs as both background information and as a presenting problem when students seek help at student counseling centers (Floerchinger, 1991), and results from pilot studies with support group interventions and counseling groups indicate, albeit tentatively, positive effects in the lives of bereaved students (Balk, Tyson-Rawson, and Colletti-Wetzel, 1993; Berson, 1988; Dodd, 1988; Janowiak, Mei-Tal, and Drapkin, 1995). These interventions need to be studied with randomized clinical trials and must respond to the concern in some circles that interventions to assist the normally bereaved are in reality unpredictable: beneficial for some persons, negligible for some, and potentially harmful for others (Jordan and Neimeyer, 2003). Questions about the effectiveness of grief counseling with the normally bereaved are based on inadequate analytical techniques and on faulty data, and clinical experience in a variety of settings supports the value of grief counseling with the normally bereaved (Larson and Hoyt, 2007a, 2007b).

Recommendations

I have four recommendations for addressing the legitimate question "So what?" when university faculty and administrators learn the prevalence rate of bereavement among college students. My recommendations focus on (1) research programs; (2) a center for bereavement research, intervention, and education; (3) review of bereavement response efforts on campuses; and (4) assessment of bereaved students' needs.

Research Programs. I recommend studies using carefully designed stratified random sampling to examine the assertions that have come mostly from convenience sampling. Will the 22 to 30 percent prevalence rate hold up to better research design? We need longitudinal research to follow the trajectory of bereavement among college students; we need to overcome the reliance on cross-sectional studies. We could test, for instance, whether student bereavement trajectories form the three distinct patterns Bonanno (2006) has reported: resilience for most, recovery for a large plurality, and extended distress for a small minority. Research is one of the core values of the university, and rigorous research on college student bereavement speaks directly to what matters at a university.

Campus-Based Bereavement Center. A campus center devoted to bereavement research, intervention, and education should be established with links to college students, alumni, faculty, administrators, and the wider community. The center's mission would be threefold: to discover knowledge about bereavement; to design, implement, and evaluate the effectiveness of interventions to assist the bereaved; and to educate about bereavement. The center would address major university goals: producing substantive scholarship, gaining notable extramural funding for sponsored programs, developing efficacious interventions and taking them to multiple sites, and engaging in partnerships with diverse stakeholders in the communities both on and beyond the campus.

One crucial task such a center can accomplish (in consort with university administrators) is to develop guidelines that require that campus counseling staff be trained in the treatment of grief, with professional workshops offered at the center. Although making referrals to counseling center staff is frequently the first suggestion to address the needs of bereaved students, skepticism among grief counseling practitioners whom I know are skeptical that most counseling center staff members are sufficiently and appropriately prepared to understand and deal with the issues presented in bereavement.

Part of preparing counseling center staff to deal with students' bereavement can consist of helping staff develop techniques for collecting loss histories from students. As mentioned earlier, experiences with loss—including divorce, breakups, and other nondeath losses—form the backstory of many students' lives. Tamina Toray informed me that in her experience, "Although the student's presenting problem may not focus on a current or past loss, such losses may have important ties or clues to the current issue facing the student, and thus it is worth the effort of ascertaining such connections."

Conversations with students have taught me that even if they would never consider going to a counseling center for help, they are willing to talk informally with an interested and informed peer. The center can develop a curriculum to train students to become peer counselors who would be given certificates upon completing the curriculum. The university can advertise the peer counseling program and make available a list of peer counselors for students to contact informally.

The bereavement center can examine its offerings by commissioning evaluations to examine the full range of programs the center offers (Stake, 2004). It can then use the findings to make appropriate adjustments to these programs. In addition, as Jeffrey Kauffman pointed out to me, by including a clear action plan examining intervention efforts, the center will not need to do the research first as to what is the best intervention strategy, because service delivery will have a research component, making the practical services the centerpiece.

Review of Bereavement Assistance Efforts on Campuses. Two examples of university responses that readily come to mind are Georgetown University's student-led efforts to provide assistance to bereaved students and the efforts at the University of Western Sydney to put in place a planned, responsive, structured approach when a student dies.

Georgetown University's efforts are called the National Students of Ailing Mothers and Fathers (AMF) Support Network. The organization's Web site (http://www.StudentsofAMF.org) states that its "mission is to support all grieving college students, empower all college students to get involved in service, and raise awareness about the needs of grieving college students." The organization has obtained wide institutional and even national support. What is impressive is both that the organization has maintained systemwide involvement and that it began as a grassroots movement inspired by the desire of bereaved students to make a difference. It has been addressing head-on the "So what?" response by interacting with college administrators and bereavement professionals across the country (Fajgenbaum and Chesson, 2007).

The University of Western Sydney (UWS) developed its Student Death Response Plan (SDRP) to provide a structured protocol detailing what the university needs to do after a student dies (Cusick, 2007). The SDRP acknowledges the efforts at such places as the University of Minnesota (Rickgarn, 1987, 1996) in which selected teams of individuals sensitive to the needs of the bereaved are mobilized on campus when a student dies, but UWS counters that an institutionwide, coordinated response is needed because "the student is a member of a complex, highly regulated, strategically driven organization" and therefore a student's death "needs a multifaceted, coordinated and targeted institutional response that may go well beyond the scope of a dedicated team" (Cusick, 2007, p. 4). Wrenn's pioneering work (1991) at the University of Arizona is credited for its seminal influence on the plans devised by the UWS.

Both the efforts at Georgetown and the efforts at UWS exemplify significant responses to the organizational mission and goals of the higher education institution. Somehow these specific responses to death and bereavement on a university campus have found ways that speak to the core of each institution. Involving these universities systemwide addresses directly the "So what?" question not by arguing that university engagement is the altruistic or sensitive thing to do but rather by framing the university's involvement within the central mission of an institution of higher education: to reach out compassionately when life crises obstruct individuals and groups from engaging in the academic and scholarly *raison d'être* for the university (Balk, 2001; Pelikan, 1993).

Needs Assessment. What has not been discussed in this chapter but is a logical next step is determining what bereaved college students need and asking whether colleges should play a central role in meeting the needs of bereaved students. Needs assessments should take into account the empirical findings calling into question whether interventions assist the normally bereaved (Jordan and Neimeyer, 2003, 2007).

1. Rather than deciding that bereaved college students are on their own and merely wishing them good luck, we should make the effort to determine whether appropriate institutional responses can be put in place to help students get beyond a life event that can obstruct their best academic performance and may ultimately affect a school's retention and graduation rates (Balk, 2001; Servaty-Seib and Hamilton, 2006). As Tamina Toray told me, "Referral to appropriate student services offices can provide grieving students much needed information to help them cope with their grief. Making academic changes such as dropping a course after deadlines have passed requires permission from the registrar or dean of student's office. There are times when a complete yet temporary break from the rigor of academia (medical withdrawal) is needed by bereaved students, yet these students are often so overwhelmed by their loss that they simply walk away from their classes, leaving a record of failing grades to contend with upon return. Often bereaved students are unaware of such policies that can lighten their load or are too overwhelmed to take the necessary steps to implement them."

NEW DIRECTIONS FOR STUDENT SERVICES • DOI: 10.1002/ss

2. Rather than bemoaning the lack of coordinated institutional responses to help bereaved students, we should determine what efforts, if any, will be of help.

3. We should ground needs assessment of bereaved students in the overall context of the university's mission and assess how such university engagement will benefit both the students and the university.

4. We should establish regular means to identify bereaved students. Jeffrey Kauffman suggested to me administering brief questionnaires during orientation, including the question "Have you experienced the death of anyone close to you in the past year (or two years)?" Combining such assessment with an educational component about mourning could help remove the stigma associated with bereavement and normalize the grief process so that students feel more comfortable seeking services.

References

Attig, T. *How We Grieve: Relearning the World.* New York: Oxford University Press, 1996.

Balk, D. E. "Death, Bereavement, and College Students: A Descriptive Analysis." *Mortality,* 1997, *2,* 207–220.

Balk, D. E. "College Student Bereavement, Scholarship, and the University: A Call for University Engagement." *Death Studies,* 2001, *25,* 67–84.

Balk, D. E., Tyson-Rawson, K., and Colletti-Wetzel, J. "Social Support as an Intervention with Bereaved College Students." *Death Studies,* 1993, *17,* 427–450.

Balk, D. E., and Vesta, L. C. "Psychological Development During Four Years of Bereavement: A Case Study." *Death Studies,* 1998, *22,* 3–21.

Berson, R. J. "A Bereavement Group for College Students." *Journal of American College Health,* 1988, *37,* 101–108.

Bonanno, G. A. "Research That Matters—2006: New Findings on Loss and Human Resilience." Symposium presented at the 28th annual conference of the Association for Death and Education and Counseling, Tampa, Fla., Mar. 29–Apr. 2, 2006.

Bowlby, J. *Attachment and Loss,* Vol. 3: *Loss.* New York: Basic Books, 1980.

Cusick, A. "Death Response Plans in Universities: A Structural Approach." Unpublished manuscript, 2007.

Dodd, D. K. "Responding to the Bereaved: A Student Panel Discussion." *Teaching of Psychology,* 1988, *15,* 33–36.

Fajgenbaum, D. C., and Chesson, B. C. "Grieving College Students: The Problems and a Solution." Paper presented at the 29th annual conference of the Association for Death Education and Counseling, Indianapolis, Ind., Apr. 15, 2007.

Floerchinger, D. S. "Bereavement in Late Adolescence: Interventions on College Campuses." *Journal of Adolescent Research,* 1991, *6,* 146–156.

Freud, S. "Mourning and Melancholia." In J. Strachey (ed. and trans.), *The Complete Psychological Works of Sigmund Freud,* Vol. 14. London: Hogarth Press, 1957. (Originally published 1917.)

Haas, A. P. "Identifying and Treating Students at Risk for Suicide: The AFSP College Screening Project." Presentation at the Suicide Prevention Research Center Discussion Series on Suicide Prevention, New York, 2004.

Hardison, H. G., Neimeyer, R. A., and Lichstein, K. L. "Insomnia and Complicated Grief Symptoms in Bereaved College Students." *Behavioral Sleep Medicine,* 2005, *3,* 99–111.

Hingson, R. W., Heeren, T., Winter, M., and Wechsler, H. "Magnitude of School-Related Mortality and Morbidity Among U.S. College Students Ages 18–24: Changes from 1998 to 2001." *Annual Review of Public Health,* 2005, *26,* 259–279.

Hingson, R. W., and others. "Magnitude of School-Related Mortality and Morbidity Among U.S. College Students Ages 18–24." *Journal of Studies on Alcohol,* 2002, *63,* 136–144.

Janowiak, S. M., Mei-Tal, R., and Drapkin, R. G. "Living with Loss: A Group for Bereaved College Students." *Death Studies,* 1995, *19,* 55–63.

Jordan, J. R., and Neimeyer, R. A. "Does Grief Counseling Work?" *Death Studies,* 2003, *27,* 765–786.

Jordan, J. R., and Neimeyer, R. A. "Historical and Contemporary Perspectives on Assessment and Intervention." In D. E. Balk, C. Wogrin, G. Thornton, and D. Meagher (eds.), *Handbook of Thanatology: The Essential Body of Knowledge for the Study of Death, Dying, and Bereavement.* River Forest, Ill.: ADEC, 2007.

King, A. R. "Family Environment Scale Predictors of Academic Performance." *Psychological Reports,* 1998, *83,* 1319–1327.

Klass, D., Silverman, P. R., and Nickman, S. L. (eds.). *Continuing Bonds: New Understandings of Grief.* Philadelphia: Taylor & Francis, 1996.

LaGrand, L. E. "College Student Loss and Response." In E. S. Zinner (ed.), *Coping with Death on Campus.* New Directions for Student Services, no. 31. San Francisco: Jossey-Bass, 1985.

LaGrand, L. E. *Coping with Separation and Loss as a Young Adult: Theoretical and Practical Realities.* Springfield, Ill.: Thomas, 1986.

Larson, D. G., and Hoyt, W. T. "The Bright Side of Grief Counseling: Deconstructing the New Pessimism." In K. J. Doka (ed.), *Living with Grief: Before and After the Death.* Washington, D.C.: Hospice Foundation of America, 2007a.

Larson, D. G., and Hoyt, W. T. "What Has Become of Grief Counseling? An Evaluation of the Empirical Foundations of the New Pessimism." *Professional Psychology: Research and Practice,* 2007b, *38,* 347–355.

Lindemann, E. "Symptomatology and Management of Acute Grief." *American Journal of Psychiatry,* 1944, *101,* 141–148.

Neimeyer, R. A., Prigerson, H. G., and Davies, B. "Mourning and Meaning." *American Behavioral Scientist,* 2002, *46,* 236–251.

Oltjenbruns, K. A. "Death of a Friend During Adolescence: Issues and Impacts." In C. A. Corr and D. E. Balk (eds.), *Handbook of Adolescent Death and Bereavement.* New York: Springer, 1996.

Park, C. L. "Religion as a Meaning-Making Framework in Coping with Life Stress." *Journal of Social Issues,* 2005, *61,* 707–729.

Pelikan, J. *The Idea of a University: A Reexamination.* New Haven, Conn.: Yale University Press, 1993.

Rickgarn, R.L.V. "The Death Response Team: Responding to the Forgotten Grievers." *Journal of Counseling and Development,* 1987, *66,* 24–40.

Rickgarn, R.L.V. "The Need for Postvention of College Campuses: A Rationale and Case Study Findings." In C. A. Corr and D. E. Balk (eds.), *Handbook of Adolescent Death and Bereavement.* New York: Springer, 1996.

Servaty-Seib, H. L., and Hamilton, L. A. "Educational Performance and Persistence of Bereaved College Students." *Journal of College Student Development,* 2006, *47,* 225–234.

Stake, R. E. *Standards-Based and Responsive Evaluation.* Thousand Oaks, Calif.: Sage, 2004.

Wrenn, R. "College Management of Student Death: A Survey." *Death Studies,* 1991, *15,* 395–402.

DAVID E. BALK is a professor in the Department of Health and Nutrition Sciences at Brooklyn College of the City University of New York and director of the Department's Graduate Studies in Thanatology program.

NEW DIRECTIONS FOR STUDENT SERVICES • DOI: 10.1002/ss

2

Theories of college student development and campus ecology provide helpful perspectives on how students cope with bereavement.

Developmental and Contextual Perspectives on Bereaved College Students

Deborah J. Taub, Heather L. Servaty-Seib

How students cope with the death of someone close to them is tied to their unique developmental status, the climate of the campus, and their personal characteristics. This chapter uses student development theory as a lens through which to consider the ways in which college students respond to and cope with death losses. Both psychosocial theory (Chickering and Reisser, 1993; Schlossberg, Waters, and Goodman, 1995) and cognitive-structural theory (Baxter Magolda, 1992; Belenky, Clinchy, Goldberger, and Tarule, 1986; Perry, 1968) are used. We also draw on campus ecology perspectives (Strange and Banning, 2001) to describe why college campuses are not supportive environments for bereaved students. The chapter concludes with recommendations for helping students cope with loss.

Developmental Perspectives

Psychosocial Development Theories. Psychosocial theories deal with the tasks that individuals face as they develop. Erikson (1959) asserted that each psychosocial developmental stage or task arises as a result of the intersection of intrapersonal changes (such as physical or biological and cognitive or psychological maturation) and environmental and social demands and expectations. Erikson identified the establishment of identity as the central developmental task of the traditional college years.

Chickering (1969) created a model of psychosocial development to address the complexity of Erikson's theory and provide greater specificity and concreteness to the concept of establishing identity. He identified psychosocial tasks (called "vectors") of the college years: developing competence (intellectual, social and interpersonal, and physical and manual), managing emotions, moving through autonomy toward interdependence, developing mature interpersonal relationships, establishing identity, developing integrity, and developing purpose (Chickering and Reisser, 1993). In this model, as in Erikson's, the overarching task is identity development.

Although Chickering's model was developed to describe the development of "traditional-age" college students (individuals between eighteen and twenty-three years of age), the developmental concepts are not exclusive to them (Chickering and Reisser, 1993; Krager, Wrenn, and Hirt, 1990). Chickering and Reisser's 1993 revision of the model extended its application to older adults and added statements from adult learners and graduate students to illustrate the vectors. Furthermore, life events, such as beginning college or graduate school or the death of a loved one, can cause individuals to "recycle" developmental themes or stages (Krager, Wrenn, and Hirt, 1990, p. 41).

How students respond to the death of someone close to them and cope with bereavement differs based on where they are in terms of these developmental tasks. For example, some bereaved students experience a decrease in their academic performance (Servaty-Seib and Hamilton, 2006); students working on achieving intellectual competence may be particularly vulnerable to having bereavement diminish their academic performance, as they may not have developed adequate study skills and strategies or the fundamental knowledge base on which their courses rest. Students working to develop interpersonal competence may lack the skills to communicate their situation and needs to others and may also lack a network of friends who could provide support. Catlin (1993) reported that some bereaved students experienced a negative change in liking and trust for others, which would complicate the development of interpersonal competence. The experience of bereavement may seem particularly overwhelming to students who have not developed an overall sense of competence; they may feel unable to deal with this loss.

Students learning to manage emotions may have difficulty identifying and accepting their intense and sometimes conflicting emotional responses (Roy, 1986), including such common emotional reactions as depression, emptiness, anger, loneliness, guilt, and fear (Balk, 1997; LaGrand, 1981, 1985; Sklar and Hartley, 1990). They may also experience difficulty finding appropriate ways to express and act on these feelings. Therefore, students may act in inappropriate ways, including repression of feelings or increased use of alcohol and other drugs (LaGrand, 1985).

Chickering and Reisser (1993) described the process of achieving emotional independence (for traditional-age students) as occurring in stages in which the student moves from dependence on parents through dependence on peers and nonparental adults to independence and then to a recognition of interdependence. Therefore, students who have not achieved emotional independence may keenly feel the loss of someone on whom they depended for reassurance and emotional support, who might be, depending on where the student is in the process, a parent, an adviser, a faculty member, a peer, or a romantic partner.

Students who have not achieved instrumental independence, the ability to carry out tasks and solve problems independently, may feel particularly bereft if they have lost a person on whose assistance they depended. They may, for example, have difficulty dealing with the tasks associated with the loss, ranging from those directly related to the death (such as the funeral) to those that are secondary to the loss (such as completing their own financial aid forms).

The process of developing mature interpersonal relationships involves growing openness and acceptance of others and development of the capacity for intimacy (Chickering and Reisser, 1993). The shift in quality of relationships that is a component of this vector is a shift to a relationship that can survive distance, separation, and crises and is characterized by balanced interdependence. Students who have not achieved this mature interdependence with partners and close friends may be inclined, in the face of a death loss, to cling to their partners and close friends or to withdraw from them. Research indicates that bereaved college students may move quickly into romantic relationships or be overly hesitant regarding them (Hepworth, Ryder, and Dreyer, 1984; Silverman, 1987). In addition, because maintaining connections with the deceased can be an important part of coping with grief and bereavement (Field, 2006; Malkinson, Rubin, and Witztum, 2006), students whose developmental status makes this difficult may experience more problematic grief.

Because each of these vectors is seen as a necessary precursor to establishing identity, difficulties in achieving these vectors may result in difficulties in establishing identity. Neimeyer (2001) argued that making meaning out of the death is *the* central process of grieving. Neimeyer and Anderson (2002) organized meaning-making into three major processes: sense-making, benefit-finding, and identity reconstruction. The third process—identity reconstruction—is of most relevance to the vector of establishing identity. The experience of a death loss disrupts one's sense of self and of one's place in the world. How can those who are still searching for who they are *reconstruct* their still-emerging sense of self, their understanding of how the world works, and their life narrative?

The vector of developing purpose involves creating plans that balance vocational interests, avocational interests, and family and lifestyle commitments (Chickering and Reisser, 1993). Research suggests that students who have not developed a general purpose in life tend to experience more difficulties with grief and bereavement, including higher grief intensity and more intrusive grief symptoms (Edmonds and Hooker, 1992; Pfost, Stevens, and Wessels, 1989; Schwartzberg and Janoff-Bulman, 1991;

Stevens, Pfost, and Wessels, 1987). The death of a close family member or partner may complicate development along this vector as a student may struggle to accommodate new and unanticipated family commitments following the death of a parent, for instance, or the need to revise plans that included the partner. In the aftermath of a significant death loss, students may reconsider their chosen paths, committing to a major field of study because of a perception that that is what the deceased would have wanted or abandoning a path that seems irrelevant after the person to whom it was important is dead.

In the vector of developing integrity (Chickering and Reisser, 1993), students move from a rigid application of moral principles to a more nuanced value system, adopt personal values, and progress toward consistency between their actions and the values they espouse. Because many bereaved students report using religious or philosophical beliefs to cope with a death loss (Park, 2005), students' progress in developing integrity can have important implications. In fact, religious issues are often connected to how the bereaved attempt to make sense of their experiences (Neimeyer and Anderson, 2002).

College students are typically people in transition—transition into college, into major fields, out of college, and so on. A significant death loss may precipitate an additional transition process for a student. Transition theory (Schlossberg, Waters, and Goodman, 1995), developed on populations of adults, focuses on the factors that influence an individual's ability to cope with transitions. Schlossberg and colleagues organized these factors into four sets: situation, self, support, and strategies. Situation factors such as timing, concurrent stressors, prior loss experiences, and role changes related to the death loss contribute to how well the individual copes with loss. For example, these researchers talked about things happening "on time" or "off time." A death might be viewed as "on time," for instance, if the deceased was elderly and in poor health, whereas the death of a young person might be viewed as "off time" (Rando, 1984).

Self factors include demographic factors (gender, age, race or ethnicity), developmental status, and psychological resources. The amount and type of social support available to the individual contribute to how well he or she copes with the transition. Unfortunately, research suggests that bereaved students do not perceive their peers as supportive (Balk, 1997; Silverman, 1987). Schlossberg and colleagues (1995) suggest that individuals who use a variety of coping strategies are most effective at coping with transitions. Seeking counseling, for example, could be seen as a *strategy* of accessing a source of *support*. However, relatively few bereaved students seek the help of counselors to cope with their grief (Balk, 1997).

Cognitive-Structural Development Theories. Whereas theorists such as Chickering (1969; Chickering and Reisser, 1993) and Schlossberg and colleagues (1995) focus on the psychosocial and identity aspects of college student development, cognitive-structural theorists focus on college students' cognitive development. How students think in general has implications for how they think about death and bereavement. How bereaved students view and interpret their situation influences how they respond and cope. Several theorists (including Baxter Magolda, 1992, 2001; Belenky, Clinchy, Goldberger, and Tarule, 1986; Perry, 1968) have addressed college students' cognitive development (both Baxter Magolda's and Perry's work was based on traditional-age college students; Belenky and her colleagues included older adult women and women outside higher education). Because the cognitive structures described by these theorists are similar (Evans, Forney, and Guido-DiBrito, 1998) and because the others' work grew out of Perry's (Love and Guthrie, 1999), we use Perry as the primary illustration of how students' bereavement may be influenced by their cognitive developmental status. We include insights from the work of Baxter Magolda and of Belenky and colleagues where relevant.

Perry's model (1968) describes students' movement from a dualistic way of thinking to an acknowledgment of multiple viewpoints to an ability to weigh evidence to support the validity of viewpoints. Perry's scheme of intellectual and ethical development culminates in students' recognition of themselves as active agents in an unfolding series of commitments and the consequences of those commitments. Dualistic thinkers see things in a dichotomous way, believe that there is a single correct answer for every question, and view themselves in passive roles as learners. Students whose thinking would be characterized by "multiplicity" in the Perry scheme are focused on fairness; they view all opinions as equally valid and regard all points of view, in the absence of proven facts, as opinions. Students whose thinking is in "relativism" use standards of evidence to judge and support arguments and display critical thinking skills. The movement from dualistic to relativistic thinking also involves movement from a primarily external locus of control (with a focus on authorities as the source of knowledge) to a primarily internal locus of control. The final positions in Perry's scheme do not involve any changes in cognitive structures; the attention shifts from intellectual development to the development of commitments, which, Perry notes, form students' sense of identity. Research within the Perry framework has found that few students graduate from college having reached the commitment positions of the Perry scheme (Baxter Magolda, 2001; Belenky, Clinchy, Goldberger, and Tarule, 1986; King and Kitchener, 1994; Love and Guthrie, 1999).

Students who think dualistically are particularly vulnerable to the notion that there is one correct way to respond to a death. Peers and others may criticize the bereaved student's ways of coping as not being the "right" or "appropriate" way to respond. Students who think dualistically may internalize these messages that they are grieving incorrectly, which can exacerbate feelings of incompetence.

Although Neimeyer (2001) has cautioned against viewing the process of finding meaning as a purely cognitive process, the ability of bereaved students to engage in productive meaning-making is influenced by their level of cognitive development. Because the process of finding meaning can be a highly individual process, it could be difficult for persons who look toward external authorities for knowledge to engage in meaning-making.

The first dimension of meaning-making (Neimeyer and Anderson, 2002), sense-making, involves finding an explanation for the death ("Why?"); although they acknowledge that making sense of the death is an ongoing process, Neimeyer and Anderson consider sense-making to be particularly important early in the grief process. Students who think dualistically seek "right" answers from authorities; those who think at somewhat more advanced levels will turn to authorities for the right *process*. If bereaved students receive some kind of answer to "Why?" from some authority, they may not be inclined to search further, accepting the "right" answer they have received.

The second dimension of meaning-making, benefit-finding, involves identifying personal, philosophical, or spiritual benefits associated with the bereavement (Neimeyer and Anderson, 2002). Finding benefits in a negative event may be beyond the comprehension of students who think dualistically. Neimeyer and Anderson's ongoing work suggests that significantly fewer bereaved traditional-age college students (in contrast to bereaved adults) are able to find even one benefit following a death loss experience.

The third dimension of meaning-making, identity reconstruction, seems particularly challenging for individuals who have not yet established their identities. Those who seek and are able to find meaning in their death losses appear to function more effectively than those who cannot find meaning (Holland, Currier, and Neimeyer, 2006; Neimeyer, Baldwin, and Gillies, 2006). Students reasoning at the earlier stages of Perry's scheme may experience more problematic adjustment than those whose thinking is more cognitively complex.

The College Environment

Theories of campus ecology (Strange and Banning, 2001) describe the reciprocal influence of students and the campus environment on one another. Strange and Banning describe the significant roles that campus environments can play in promoting and enhancing students' adjustment, development, learning, and success. Because campuses are also places in which bereaved students may grieve their death losses, it is important to examine these environments and their impact.

Colleges are unique environments for a number of reasons, many of which have to do with the human aggregate—the people who inhabit and therefore define the character of the environment (Strange and Banning, 2001). The college setting can be overwhelmingly young; on residential campuses in particular, traditional-age students are surrounded by large numbers of their peers in the classroom, on campus, and where they live. On these campuses especially, student contact with young children and the elderly tends to be lacking, and students encounter adults mostly at a distance—as classroom instructors, for example.

The residential college environment is focused on activity, sociability, and fun (Howe and Strauss, 2003; Nathan, 2005). College students tend to be busy people, packing their lives with a variety of extracurricular activities. The pervasive atmosphere is often one of pressure on the one hand and partying on the other—"working hard and playing hard." Grieving students can feel excluded in this environment.

For many traditional-age students, the fun atmosphere of college involves alcohol. The Harvard School of Public Health College Alcohol Study found that 44.4 percent of college students were binge drinkers (Wechsler and others, 2002) and that this rate of binge drinking had remained stable over eight years of study. Kadison and DiGeronimo (2004) asserted that drinking in college has become glamorized as a rite of passage, inextricably linked with the college experience for many students. It is not surprising, therefore, that many bereaved college students turn to alcohol and the use of other drugs in an attempt to cope with their grief (LaGrand, 1985).

College students also face almost constant academic pressure. A recent American College Health Association National College Health Assessment indicated that 94 percent of college student respondents reported that they felt overwhelmed at times (Kisch, Leino, and Silverman, 2005). This ever-present pressure makes the college campus a difficult environment in which to grieve. Physical symptoms (such as headaches, exhaustion, and insomnia) and psychological symptoms of grief can affect students' ability to concentrate, study, or attend class (Hardison, Neimeyer, and Lichstein, 2005; Oltjenbruns, 1998). Academic pressure can add to the difficulty bereaved students might have asking faculty members for extensions to deadlines, makeup exams, or grades of "incomplete." As a result, college might not feel safe for bereaved students.

Chickering (1969) identified the peer culture as the most powerful influence on students' development. Bereaved students have reported a lack of supportive peers (Balk, 1997; Silverman, 1987). In fact, bereaved students reported that their peers were uncomfortable discussing the topic of grief (Balk, 1997) or communicated the need for the bereaved to "get over it" (Silverman, 1987, p. 393). These responses by peers can further isolate grieving students, exacerbating their feelings of being alone in an environment where others do not share their feelings.

How Institutions of Higher Education Can Assist Bereaved Students

Higher education institutions can and should support bereaved students. Training can provide campus professionals and paraprofessionals with increased knowledge about grief and ways to respond to grieving students. Such training, however, must emphasize the developmental aspects (both psychosocial and cognitive) influencing bereaved college students and environmental elements that might affect bereaved students' grief experiences. For example:

New Directions for Student Services • DOI: 10.1002/ss

• *Provide training about loss and bereavement to resident assistants* (LaGrand, 1985). Resident assistants are in an ideal position to assist residents who have experienced a significant death because they are able to observe signs of distress (crying, depression, skipping classes, and so on). Training in loss and bereavement can help RAs support bereaved residents, who too frequently find little support among their peers. Training of RAs should include information about how students' developmental status affects coping with bereavement. Chapter Five provides detailed information on designing and delivering such training.

• *Offer training about loss and bereavement to others who work closely with students, such as academic advisers, student organization advisers, student affairs professionals, and faculty* (Servaty-Seib and Hamilton, 2006; Stephenson, 1985). Both residential and commuter students, who tend to spend less time on campus than their residential counterparts, interact with faculty, advisers, and other professionals (Jacoby and Garland, 2004–2005). Campus professionals who work closely with students in all capacities can recognize that a student is struggling and can serve as someone in whom a student might confide. These professionals can also benefit from training on issues of loss and bereavement, as well as about student and adult development. Having a wide variety of people on campus who are knowledgeable about loss and bereavement can help create an environment in which bereaved students do not feel isolated or unsupported.

• *Encourage counseling center staff to gain specialized training in loss and bereavement.* Given how common bereavement among college students is, one might be surprised to know that most college counseling center staff have little or no specific training about death and bereavement (Freeman and Ward, 1998). As a result, these staff are often not equipped to be as helpful as they could be to grieving students who seek the assistance of a mental health professional. Such specialized training is available through the Association for Death Education and Counseling. Counseling center professionals also interact with a broad range of students on campus and therefore need to understand the effects of students' developmental status and age on responses to death losses.

Colleges can also offer programs to support grieving students and can develop and distribute educational materials to raise awareness among students. For instance:

• *Provide grief groups and grief workshops through the campus counseling center* (LaGrand, 1985; Vickio and Clark, 1998). Bereaved college students are likely to feel ambivalent about seeking counseling because they do not see grief as a mental health issue (Balk, 2001; Wrenn, 1999). Given that bereaved students often report finding little support among their peers, grief groups can provide a much needed opportunity for bereaved students to share feelings and experiences with, and find support from, peers who have had similar experiences. Grief workshops (see Chapter Four) are another possibility that may be attractive to students who are averse to seeking counseling. In both cases, facilitators should consider students' cognitive and psychosocial development when selecting topics and determining structure.

• *Provide educational materials to students about grief and loss that could help them support their bereaved friends* (LaGrand, 1985). Most students want to help their grieving friends but do not know how. Educational materials, including brochures, Web sites, and bulletin boards, can provide basic information about the dynamics of grief and loss and offer suggestions for assisting bereaved peers (see, for example, Rack and others, forthcoming).

Recognition of the needs of bereaved students through policies not only provides them with support but also counters the isolation they may feel (Doka, 2002) by communicating that they and their concerns matter to the college. For example:

• *Establish bereavement policies for students.* Most campuses have bereavement policies for employees, but many lack such policies for students. This puts bereaved students in the position of needing to negotiate class absences, missed assignments, makeup work, and grades of "incomplete" with individual faculty members on a course-by-course basis. Moreover, the campus culture may discourage asking for such accommodations. Bereaved students may have particular difficulty repeating their story to a series of professors and asking for help, particularly if they are struggling to develop instrumental and emotional independence (Chickering and Reisser, 1993). In the absence of such policies, students have no guarantee that accommodations will be made or any reason to expect consistent faculty responses to requests.
• *In designing policies and developing training and educational materials, be sensitive to cultural differences in grief and mourning practices, as well as to developmental differences.* As the college student population becomes increasingly diverse, campus policies must be broad enough to encompass the range of mourning practices present in a multicultural student body. Jewish tradition, for example, requires that funeral and burial take place as soon as possible following a death, preferably in the first twenty-four hours (Lamm, 2000). Therefore, a Jewish student may have little or no time to contact faculty prior to leaving campus in response to a death. Ceremonies preceding and following a Native American burial can last for several days (Adams, 1997; Manataka American Indian Council, 2006), requiring an extended absence from campus following a death. Training and educational materials should also acknowledge significant cultural differences in beliefs about death, mourning practices and length of mourning period, and expectations and duties of the bereaved (Rothaupt and Becker, 2007).

Conclusions

Because bereavement is a common experience among college students, institutions of higher education must understand how students respond to death loss to take actions to assist them appropriately. Although grief and bereavement are idiosyncratic (Rando, 1996), understanding college students' developmental status as well as the unique features of the campus environment can inform student affairs professionals in helping bereaved students. In addition, colleges and universities can provide training and implement policies to assist grieving students.

References

Adams, N. "My Grandmother and the Snake." In A. Garrod and C. Larimore (eds.), *First Person, First Peoples*. Ithaca, N.Y.: Cornell University Press, 1997.

Balk, D. E. "Death, Bereavement, and College Students: A Descriptive Analysis." *Mortality*, 1997, 2, 207–220.

Balk, D. E. "College Student Bereavement, Scholarship, and the University: A Call for University Engagement." *Death Studies*, 2001, 25, 67–84.

Baxter Magolda, M. B. *Knowing and Reasoning in College: Gender-Related Patterns in Students' Intellectual Development*. San Francisco: Jossey-Bass, 1992.

Baxter Magolda, M. B. *Making Their Own Way*. Sterling, Va.: Stylus, 2001.

Belenky, M. F., Clinchy, B. M., Goldberger, N. R., and Tarule, J. M. *Women's Ways of Knowing: The Development of Self, Voice, and Mind*. New York: Basic Books, 1986.

Catlin, G. "The Role of Culture in Grief." *Journal of Social Psychology*, 1993, 133, 173–184.

Chickering, A. W. *Education and Identity*. San Francisco: Jossey-Bass, 1969.

Chickering, A. W., and Reisser, L. *Education and Identity*. (2nd ed.). San Francisco: Jossey-Bass, 1993.

Doka, K. J. *Disenfranchised Grief: New Directions, Challenges, and Strategies for Practice*. Champaign, Ill.: Research Press, 2002.

Edmonds, S., and Hooker, K. "Perceived Changes in Life Meaning Following Bereavement." *Omega*, 1992, 25, 307–318.

Erikson, E. H. *Identity and the Life Cycle*. New York: Norton, 1959.

Evans, N. J., Forney, D. S., and Guido-DiBrito, F. *Student Development in College: Theory, Research, and Practice*. San Francisco: Jossey-Bass, 1998.

Field, N. P. "Continuing Bonds in Adaptation to Bereavement: Introduction." *Death Studies*, 2006, 30, 700–714.

Freeman, S. J., and Ward, S. "Death and Bereavement: What Counselors Should Know." *Journal of Mental Health Counseling*, 1998, 20, 213–223.

Hardison, H. G., Neimeyer, R. A., and Lichstein, K. L. "Insomnia and Complicated Grief Symptoms in Bereaved College Students." *Behavioral Sleep Medicine*, 2005, 3, 99–111.

Hepworth, J., Ryder, R. G., and Dreyer, A. S. "The Effects of Parental Loss on the Formation of Intimate Relationships." *Journal of Marital and Family Therapy*, 1984, 10, 73–82.

Holland, J. M., Currier, J. M., and Neimeyer, R. A. "Meaning Reconstruction in the First Two Years of Bereavement: The Role of Sense-Making and Benefit Finding." *Omega*, 2006, 53, 175–191.

Howe, N., and Strauss, W. *Millennials Go to College*. Washington, D.C.: American Association of Collegiate Registrars and Admissions Officers, 2003.

Jacoby, B., and Garland, J. "Strategies for Enhancing Commuter Student Success." *Journal of College Student Retention*, 2004–2005, 6, 61–79.

Kadison, R. D., and DiGeronimo, T. F. *College of the Overwhelmed: The Campus Mental Health Crisis and What to Do About It*. San Francisco: Jossey-Bass, 2004.

King, P. M., and Kitchener, K. S. *Developing Reflective Judgment: Understanding and Promoting Intellectual Growth and Critical Thinking in Adolescents and Adults.* San Francisco: Jossey-Bass, 1994.

Kisch, J., Leino, E. V., and Silverman, M. M. "Aspects of Suicidal Behavior, Depression, and Treatment in College Students: Results from the Spring 2000 National College Health Assessment Survey." *Suicide and Life-Threatening Behavior,* 2005, *35,* 3–13.

Krager, L., Wrenn, R., and Hirt, J. "Perspectives on Age Differences." In L. V. Moore (ed.), *Evolving Theoretical Perspectives on Students.* New Directions for Student Services, no. 51. San Francisco: Jossey-Bass, 1990.

LaGrand, L. E. "Loss Reactions of College Students: A Descriptive Analysis." *Death Education,* 1981, *5,* 235–248.

LaGrand, L. E. "College Student Loss and Response." In E. S. Zinner (ed.), *Coping with Death on Campus.* New Directions for Student Services, no. 31. San Francisco: Jossey-Bass, 1985.

Lamm, M. *The Jewish Way in Death and Mourning.* (rev. ed.). New York: Jonathan David, 2000.

Love, P. G., and Guthrie, V. L. "Perry's Intellectual Scheme." In P. G. Love and V. L. Guthrie (eds.), *Understanding and Applying Cognitive Developmental Theory.* New Directions for Student Services, no. 88. San Francisco: Jossey-Bass, 1999.

Malkinson, R., Rubin, S. S., and Witztum, E. "Therapeutic Issues and the Relationship to the Deceased: Working Clinically with the Two-Track Model of Bereavement." *Death Studies,* 2006, *30,* 797–815.

Manataka American Indian Council. "Native American Spirituality." [http://www.manataka.org/page1970.html]. 2006.

Nathan, R. *My Freshman Year: What a Professor Learned by Becoming a Student.* Ithaca, N.Y.: Cornell University Press, 2005.

Neimeyer, R. A. *Lessons of Loss: A Guide to Coping.* New York: Brunner-Routledge, 2001.

Neimeyer, R. A., and Anderson, A. "Meaning Reconstruction Theory." In N. Thompson (ed.), *Loss and Grief: A Guide for Human Service Practitioners.* New York: Palgrave Macmillan, 2002.

Neimeyer, R. A., Baldwin, S. A., and Gillies, J. "Continuing Bonds and Reconstructing Meaning: Mitigating Complications in Bereavement." *Death Studies,* 2006, *30,* 715–738.

Oltjenbruns, K. A. "Ethnicity and the Grief Response: Mexican Americans Versus Anglo American College Students." *Death Studies,* 1998, *22,* 141–155.

Park, C. L. "Religion as a Meaning-Making Framework in Coping with Life Stress." *Journal of Social Issues,* 2005, *61,* 707–729.

Perry, W. G., Jr. *Forms of Intellectual and Ethical Development in the College Years: A Scheme.* Austin, Tex.: Holt, Rinehart and Winston, 1968.

Pfost, K. S., Stevens, M. J., and Wessels, A. B. "Relationship of Purpose in Life to Grief Experiences in Response to the Death of a Significant Other." *Death Studies,* 1989, *13,* 371–378.

Rack, J. J., and others. "Bereaved Adults' Evaluations of Grief Management Messages: Effects of Message Person Centeredness, Recipient Individual Differences, and Contextual Factors." *Death Studies,* forthcoming.

Rando, T. A. *Grief, Dying, and Death: Clinical Interventions for Caregivers.* Champaign, Ill.: Research Press, 1984.

Rando, T. A. "Grief and Mourning: Accommodation to Loss." In H. Wass and R. A. Neimeyer (eds.), *Dying: Facing the Facts.* Philadelphia: Taylor & Francis, 1995.

Rothaupt, J. W., and Becker, K. "A Literature Review of Western Bereavement Theory: From Decathecting to Continuing Bonds." *Family Journal,* 2007, *15,* 6–15.

Roy, E. T. "Treating the Grieving Student." In J. E. Talley and W.J.K. Rockwell (eds.), *Counseling and Psychotherapy with College Students: A Guide to Treatment.* New York: Praeger, 1986.

Schlossberg, N. K, Waters, E. B., and Goodman, J. *Counseling Adults in Transition.* (2nd ed.). New York: Springer, 1995.

Schwartzberg, S. S., and Janoff-Bulman, R. "Grief and the Search for Meaning: Exploring the Assumptive Worlds of Bereaved College Students." *Journal of Social and Clinical Psychology,* 1991, *10,* 270–288.

Servaty-Seib, H. L., and Hamilton, L. A. "Educational Attainment and Persistence of Bereaved College Students." *Journal of College Student Development,* 2006, *47,* 225–234.

Silverman, P. R. "The Impact of Parental Death on College-Age Women." *Psychiatric Clinics of North America,* 1987, *10,* 387–404.

Sklar, F., and Hartley, S. F. "Close Friends as Survivors: Bereavement Patterns in a 'Hidden' Population." *Omega,* 1990, *21,* 103–112.

Stephenson, J. S. "Death and the Campus Community: Organizational Realities and Personal Tragedies." In E. S. Zinner (ed.), *Coping with Death on Campus.* New Directions in Student Services, no. 31. San Francisco: Jossey-Bass, 1985.

Stevens, M. J., Pfost, K. S., and Wessels, A. B. "The Relationship of Purpose in Life to Coping Strategies and Time Since Death of a Significant Other." *Journal of Counseling and Development,* 1987, *65,* 424–426.

Strange, C. C., and Banning, J. H. *Educating by Design: Creating Campus Learning Environments That Work.* San Francisco: Jossey-Bass, 2001.

Vickio, C. J., and Clark, C. A. "Growing Through Grief: A Psychoeducational Workshop Series for Bereaved Students." *Journal of College Student Development,* 1998, *39,* 621–623.

Wechsler, H., and others. "Trends in College Binge Drinking During a Period of Increased Prevention Efforts: Findings from Four Harvard School of Public Health College Alcohol Study Surveys, 1993–2001." *Journal of American College Health,* 2002, *50,* 203–217.

Wrenn, R. L. "The Grieving College Student." In J. D. Davidson and K. J. Doka (eds.), *Living with Grief: At Work, at School, at Worship.* New York: Brunner-Routledge, 1999.

DEBORAH J. TAUB *is associate professor of higher education and coordinator of the Higher Education program, Department of Curriculum and Instruction at the University of North Carolina at Greensboro.*

HEATHER L. SERVATY-SEIB *is associate professor of educational studies at Purdue University, first vice-president of the Association for Death Education, and a counseling psychologist in private practice.*

3

The authors discuss lessons from a multifaceted research program focused on how individuals find meaning in the wake of loss experiences. These lessons offer guidance to help bereaved students make sense of bereavement and move beyond grief to growth.

Lessons of Loss: Meaning-Making in Bereaved College Students

Robert A. Neimeyer, Anna Laurie, Tara Mehta, Heather Hardison, Joseph M. Currier

Toward the end of the fall semester, Tom receives a call from home informing him that the car belonging to his depressed uncle has been found on a bridge near town with the keys still in the ignition. As Tom struggles to concentrate on final exams and as police dredge the river for his uncle's body, Tom turns to trusted professors for reading materials to help him and his family make sense of this tragic death and grapple with their traumatic grief constructively.

Following the murder of a teammate, the eighteen members of a women's athletic team accept the recommendation of their coach to attend a meeting with a male and a female counselor. The students' responses are as diverse as their ethnicities and cultures—some eulogizing their friend, some voicing their pain and fear through tears and choking sobs, some expressing their guilt for allowing their friend to drift into "the wrong crowd," some remaining stoic, and most expressing rage at the suspected killer. While helping students share these feelings and encouraging them to use the group to address their common concerns, the counselors answer the women's questions regarding the nature of the death whenever possible and suggest strategies for managing their grief. They conclude by offering another meeting in one month for those who are interested.

WILEY
InterScience®
DISCOVER SOMETHING GREAT

NEW DIRECTIONS FOR STUDENT SERVICES, no. 121, Spring 2008 © Wiley Periodicals, Inc.
Published online in Wiley InterScience (www.interscience.wiley.com) • DOI: 10.1002/ss.264

Jill, a student in her early thirties, seeks services at the university counseling center nine months after the "horrendous" death of her mother as a consequence of lifelong alcohol abuse. Compounding her acute grief over the death is a powerful sense of guilt from her failure to respond to her mother's attempts to draw closer as her life-threatening liver disease worsened and as Jill's partner, Kendra, demanded that she distance herself from her "pathological family." Jill's mother died alone, and Jill is left feeling that much between them was left unsaid. With her grades slipping, her sense of isolation from friends and family growing, and her own reliance on alcohol increasing, Jill is desperate to break out of the cycle in which she feels trapped before she "repeats Mom's life story."

These scenarios represent only three of the countless ways death can enter the lives of college students of all ages, sometimes foreshadowed by grim anticipation, though often sudden. Indeed, the rates of college student bereavement indicated in our own research (Hardison, Neimeyer, and Lichstein, 2005) converges with that of others (Balk, 2001) to suggest that approximately 25 percent of college students have lost a significant family member or friend in the past year and nearly 50 percent have suffered a loss in the past two years. If only because the prevalence of such loss is matched by widespread inattention to this stressful life transition (Balk, 2001), bereavement might be regarded as a "silent epidemic" on campus, one that can have adverse consequences for how students engage the academic, social, and developmental challenges of college. In this chapter, we offer concrete suggestions, based on our extensive research on bereaved students, to support such students, with a special emphasis on students' attempts to revise their understanding of the world now that their outlook has been shaken by tragic loss.

When Grief Is Complicated

Bereavement is a normal life transition and one that most survivors meet with resilience and constructive forms of coping (Bonanno, 2004). Although grief is never simple or easy, we must distinguish between the normative experience of most bereaved individuals and "complicated grief," a specific psychological condition under consideration for inclusion in the next revision of the *Diagnostic and Statistical Manual of Mental Disorders*. Evidence suggests that for approximately 10 to 15 percent of bereaved persons, this debilitating and prolonged form of grieving can pose severe long-term risks to their psychological and physical health through its association with generalized anxiety, depression, and stress-related diseases of the cardiovascular and immune systems (Ott, 2003; Prigerson and Maciejewski, 2006). Some of the symptoms associated with complicated bereavement or grief include yearning and pining for the deceased at least daily for months on end, difficulty accepting the death, loss of purpose, impaired functioning in life roles, and feelings of unease about moving ahead with one's life (see Zhang, El-Jawahri, and Prigerson, 2006, for complete criteria). Even in milder forms, grief complications, such as preoccupation with the death of a friend or family member, can disrupt the emotional, social, and academic functioning of college students, posing significant challenges to their successful negotiation of normal tasks of college life (Janowiak, Mei-Tal, and Drapkin, 1995).

Loss experiences such as those of the students described at the start of the chapter can challenge seriously each of the domains of students' psychosocial development (Chickering and Reisser, 1997). Bereaved students, regardless of age, seek cognitive understanding of sometimes senseless losses, struggle with the powerful emotions death engenders, confront the grief responses of others to the same loss, and seek to reestablish a sense of purpose and direction as they integrate the loss into their ongoing lives (see Chapter Two). Although most bereaved individuals surmount these hurdles (Bonanno, 2004), some will not. Therefore, college counselors, residential life staff, coaches, faculty, and administrators should be alert to symptoms of complicated grief that show little reduction across time (see Prigerson and Maciejewski, 2006).

In our research on bereaved students, we have studied a broad spectrum of concerns stemming from loss, ranging from worrisome behavioral patterns to subtle concerns about the meaning of life and spiritual issues. In one study, Hardison and her colleagues (2005) concentrated on sleep and grief-related symptoms in a cohort of more than five hundred bereaved college students. The bereaved students were more likely to meet criteria for insomnia diagnosis than a sample of three hundred nongrieving peers, a diagnosis to which those who were bereaved by the violent deaths of loved ones were particularly prone. The students who suffered violent loss were also at greater risk for complicated grief symptoms than those whose loved ones died from natural causes. Furthermore, closeness to the deceased (as assessed by the level of reported intimacy in the relationship) was associated with more symptoms of complicated grief, whereas whether or not the deceased was a family member was not. Therefore, emotionally close nonfamily losses (as of dating partners or classmates) can be as distressing to college students as the loss of kin and deserve attention by college counseling services. In addition, insomniacs in the bereaved group reported more complicated grief symptoms than the non-insomniacs, which may indicate that insomnia and complicated grief can become mutually reinforcing. Moreover, students with complicated grief symptoms and insomnia reported troubling behavior patterns, including impaired daytime functioning and reliance on alcohol and medication to induce sleep.

Because of the link between insomnia and problematic grief responses, counselors working with bereaved students should assess each client's sleep patterns. From a practical standpoint, both pharmacological and behavioral sleep interventions with bereaved students could mitigate the intensity of grief symptoms following a loss or prevent a course of normal grief from becoming protracted and complicated. In addition to using such familiar methods as relaxation training to help troubled students prepare for bedtime, a host of techniques focused on sleep enhancement—such as using

NEW DIRECTIONS FOR STUDENT SERVICES • DOI: 10.1002/ss

bedtime only for sleep and avoiding daytime napping (Lichstein, 1994)—could prove useful in breaking the cycle of recurring processing of the loss and sleeplessness. When combined with counseling and educational strategies to address grief, such sleep-restorative interventions can help students regain control of disrupted behavioral routines and take initial steps toward healthy adaptation to bereavement.

Finding Meaning Following Loss

A central theme in most of our studies of bereaved students concerns the processes by which students reassess and revise their sense of how the world works after their worldviews have been challenged by loss (Neimeyer, 2002). This approach to the life transition occasioned by the death of a loved one reflects a broader constructivist perspective in psychology (Kelly, 1955; Neimeyer and Mahoney, 1995) that views people as beings who seek to find meaning in all experiences. According to this perspective, humans strive to organize life events according to personally significant ideas so that they can understand, anticipate, and to some extent control their world. Viewed in this light, human beings' sense of self emerges from an ongoing effort to determine the meaning of life experiences in a way that is consistent with their ideas about who they were in the past and who they will be in the future. Anything that disrupts the coherence of one's self-narrative can challenge and erode not only the script by which one lives but also one's very sense of self.

The death of a loved one ranks high on the list of potentially life- and identity-changing events. Bereaved individuals, including college students, often regard the story of their lives as being demarcated by their death loss experience. Consider the comments of a college student regarding death of her mother a few years before: "[My mother's] death is the defining moment in my life. That is what defines me. . . . I am the girl whose mom died; that is me. I'd have to say that was the defining moment in all aspects. That's what changed my life. . . . It just splits your life in half from before and then after" (Schultz, 2007, p. 25).

In the immediate aftermath of the death of a friend, mentor, or family member, bereaved students often draw on spiritual or philosophic beliefs, as well as familiar relationships and routines, to find a modicum of meaning and stability in a world that has been shaken (Balk, 1997). Those who succeed in integrating the loss into their existing structures may be characterized as resilient, bouncing back relatively quickly to resume their preloss patterns and to recover their familiar sense of self (Neimeyer, 2006). But for others, such losses can overturn their taken-for-granted assumptions that the world is predictable, that the universe is benign, that important attachment relationships can be counted on, and that they are competent to face life's demands (Edmonds and Hooker, 1992). The consequence of the disruption of these assumptions (Janoff-Bulman, 1989) can be far-reaching, disorganizing not only one's routines and relationships in the present but also calling into question one's long-term plans and commitments. Under favorable circumstances, this shaking up of a stable sense of self can lead to significant growth (Calhoun and Tedeschi, 2006) as the bereaved person deepens his or her perspective on life; reviews and revises basic priorities; and grows in maturity, competence, and compassion (Neimeyer, 2004). When attempts at making sense of the loss, finding some form of silver lining in the dark cloud of bereavement, and rebuilding a sense of self without the loved one fail, however, exacerbation of distress and coping attempts marked by rigid and recurrent cycles of thought can result (Gillies and Neimeyer, 2006).

In the following sections, we discuss our research on bereaved college students with an emphasis on the practical implications of each study. We conclude with remarks on student diversity and bereavement and points to remember for counselors and other campus professionals

Violent Versus Natural Death. Even the natural and anticipated death of a significant person can be fraught with difficulty for students, who return home in midsemester for the funeral of a beloved grandmother, witness a mother's slow demise from metastatic breast cancer, or learn of an uncle's death from emphysema. But when the loss is sudden and grotesque, as through mutilating automobile accidents, suicide, or homicide, the challenge to the student's capacity to make meaning of the tragic event can be even greater. After we established the general tendency of violent death to be associated with more intense and disorganizing grief for survivors (Currier, Holland, Coleman, and Neimeyer, 2006), we turned to testing whether a student's ability or inability to make sense of the death was related to the cause of death or to common reactions associated with certain causes of death. Establishing such an association could assist individuals working with bereaved college students. If making sense of the death is a particularly salient issue for those grieving violent death losses, encouraging grieving students in their efforts to make some sort of sense of the experience could be a first step in helping them integrate the tragedy and move forward with their lives.

More than one thousand bereaved college students, nearly three hundred of whom had lost loved ones to violent forms of dying, completed a measure of complicated grief symptoms and reported how much sense they had been able to make of the loss, in whatever terms mattered to them (spiritual, philosophical, practical, and so on) (Currier, Holland, and Neimeyer, 2006). These data were analyzed to see if the more intense and debilitating grief symptoms of the members of the violent bereavement group could be explained by their failure to find meaning in the loss. This was precisely what emerged: the more problematic grief of students whose loved ones died of suicide, homicide, or accidents was nearly perfectly accounted for by the failure of their search for meaning to lead to any sustaining answers for a senseless loss. Indeed, sense-making continued to account for the uniquely complicated adjustment of this group even when compared with sudden natural death causes, as through heart attack.

These results indicate that individuals working with college students who are grieving violent deaths must consider how they can assist these students in searching for significance and meaning in the loss. For example, we have found it helpful to begin by exploring the circumstances surrounding the death, encouraging students to relate the story of the loss and others' reactions to it, in greater detail than they do in other contexts, perhaps closing their eyes to give them privacy in reliving its intensity. Such revisiting of the death, sometimes repeated across sessions, has been effective in working with students grieving traumatic deaths (Shear, Frank, Houch, and Reynolds, 2005). In addition to revisiting the experience, we recommend exploring students' processes of finding meaning by prompting them with open-ended questions:

How did you make sense of the death or loss at the time?
How do you interpret the loss now?
What philosophical or spiritual beliefs contributed to your adjustment to this loss? How were they affected by it?
Are there ways in which this loss disrupted the continuity of your life story? How, over time, have you dealt with this?

Patricia, for example, recounted her father's death by heart attack when he was helping her move into her college residence hall, focusing on his background of suspicious cardiac symptoms and the dramatic but futile attempts of the paramedics to revive him. Reflecting on the question concerning spirituality a year following his death, she noted:

> At the time of his death, I think I was much more aware of how my spiritual beliefs impacted the experience. It seemed as if my dad's body was no longer him, and in a way, it seemed like his spirit had left. Maybe the sense I had of this made it easier to deal with the burial and his no longer physical presence. My spiritual beliefs grew stronger as a result of the experience, because I was affected greatly by seeing the moment when he no longer was alive or conscious. I have less fear of death now, because my father has gone before me.

College campuses are challenged to consider institutionally based strategies for facilitating sense-making when violent deaths affect the entire campus. Memorial services, tangible markers of remembrance (such as tree plantings), and opportunities to share stories regarding those who have died may be necessary when deaths are violent. Such community-based activities may allow members in the community to establish a shared sense of meaning. Deaths, particularly when they attract considerable media atten-

When we quote students directly, we have disguised the speakers to ensure their anonymity, and the material is used with their permission.

More detailed instructions for conducting such meaning reconstruction interviews are provided elsewhere (Neimeyer, 2002), along with additional methods (such as metaphorical stories and biographical writing) to foster sense-making in the face of apparently senseless losses.

NEW DIRECTIONS FOR STUDENT SERVICES • DOI: 10.1002/ss

tion (as the 2007 shootings at Virginia Tech did), challenge the campus community's sense of its collective identity as well as individuals' sense of self.

Sense-Making Versus Benefit-Finding. As important as sense-making seems to be in bereavement adaptation, it is only one possible form of finding meaning in the wake of loss. Another is *benefit-finding,* in which bereaved people seek to grasp some positive implications of the loss. Consider, for example, the quest for some benefit in bereavement pursued by Kevin, a student whose uncle wasted away with cancer:

> It took me by surprise, his death. I have to learn to accept it though. Finding out someone close to me [died] was hard for me to accept, but I am sure it was even harder for him to know he was going to die. . . . But I still have other good times in my future. I don't think he would have wanted me to be as upset and depressed as I am. He would have wanted me to celebrate his life, not his death. . . . I just don't think I understood why he had to die. Everyone grieves in their own way.
>
> In a way, I [am] glad I realized this, so maybe I will not take life for granted all the time. It's pretty bad someone has to die to make me realize that, but I think Terry would understand. He had cancer, and he couldn't change that. The doctors couldn't. . . . It was his time, and if he accepts it, why shouldn't I? [Neimeyer and Anderson, 2002, p. 59].

This search for affirmative insights for his own life was difficult, articulated only after intensive and emotional journaling about the death some months after the loss. These insights also seemed to emerge against the backdrop of an ongoing attempt to make sense of the death and accept its finality.

Some investigators have found that benefit-finding plays a different—though complementary—role in bereavement adaptation than sense-making. Benefit-finding may in fact serve as a better predictor of adjustment in the second year of loss, when the role of sense-making has begun to diminish (Davis, Nolen-Hoeksema, and Larson, 1998). To investigate this possibility, we conducted a survey of a large number of bereaved students, aged eighteen to fifty-three, in the first two years of their grief. This project included an assessment of their ability not only to make sense of the loss but also to find some benefit in it for themselves (such as becoming a stronger person) or for others (such as ending their loved one's suffering) (Holland, Currier, and Neimeyer, 2006). Results provided only partial support for the findings of Davis and his colleagues. Students who found neither meaning nor compensatory benefit in the loss experienced the most complicated grief symptoms. Students who were able to identify some benefit, in the presence or absence of sense-making, fared better than those who did not identify some benefit. However, the best adjustment was reported by students who reported *high* degrees of sense-making but only *low* benefits in the loss. Although this result was unexpected, it might suggest that being able to integrate the death into one's life story in a way that makes it somehow understandable is more crucial than

NEW DIRECTIONS FOR STUDENT SERVICES • DOI: 10.1002/ss

finding some benefit in the experience, which might be viewed as selfish by some students. If this result is replicated by further research, it could imply a secondary role for benefit-finding in softening the impact of loss when a deeper meaning for the loss cannot be found.

Techniques for fostering benefit-finding in the wake of loss include questioning and journaling methods (Neimeyer, 2002). Counselors working with bereaved students can use these methods to assist their clients in identifying positive impacts of their losses. Counselors also can counter client's perceptions that such a search is selfish or inappropriate, perhaps by drawing attention to their greater capacity to reach out to others.

Continuing Connections. One of the more revolutionary changes in theories of grief during the past decade has been a widespread critique of the classical Freudian assumption that grieving involves a process of letting go of the one who had died to invest energy and commitment in new relationships (Klass, Silverman, and Nickman, 1996). Rather than breaking the bond with the deceased, the goal of grieving is viewed as redefining the relationship so that it can be sustained symbolically, spiritually, or in memory, through shared storytelling with family and friends, and in a host of ways that permit attachment to the deceased to remain a vital part of one's life (Attig, 1996; Hedtke and Winslade, 2003).

To examine the concept of continuing connections for bereaved college students, we conducted a study to see if bonds with the dead interacted with meaning-making to predict levels of complicated grief symptoms (Neimeyer, Baldwin, and Gillies, 2006). More than five hundred bereaved college students, ranging in age from young adulthood to midlife, completed the measure of complicated grief, reported on their level of success in making sense of their loss, and indicated the extent to which their sense of identity had changed since the loss. They also indicated if this change in identity had been for the better (for example, by becoming more compassionate or reordering life priorities) or worse (becoming more fearful or more reluctant to get close to others for fear of losing them). They also completed a measure of their continuing connection with the deceased, rating the degree to which they sought the loved one's belongings or things that reminded them of the person, had inner conversations with the individual, and so on. As one might expect, symptoms of complicated grief were greater for losses of family than nonfamily members, for those to whom students felt closer, and for students whose identity was most shaken and changed by the death. In contrast, both sense-making and benefit-finding were associated with more positive grief outcomes. Students who continued to feel attached strongly to their loved one but for whom the death made little sense experienced their loss as anguishing and intense. In contrast, even high levels of continuing connection could be managed more easily when the death could be understood within some broader framework.

Counselors seeking to explore the nature of the continuing connection with the dead loved one might make use of questions about the continuing relationship, coupled with questions about practical coping methods, sense-making, and benefit-finding. Additional techniques for exploring or strengthening a meaningful and comforting bond with the deceased include the "life imprint" method and memory books (Neimeyer, 2002).

In much the same way, educators who advise student organizations, direct living units, or work with teams in which a member has died can help grieving survivors maintain a bond with their lost colleague. Creating a memory book together, for example, could be beneficial. Students might also create a meaningful legacy or memorial for their friend, such as posting messages on the Facebook and MySpace pages of the deceased.

A Note on Diversity. We should note that nearly all research on bereavement is conducted on Caucasian populations. To help rectify this imbalance in the literature, Rosenblatt and Wallace (2005) conducted a qualitative study with a small sample of African Americans, yielding some fascinating insights about unique dimensions of their responses to bereavement as a function of a history of racism, different family structures, a strong sense of connection to the deceased, and the impact of violent death on the community. To extend these promising preliminary understandings, we assembled what we believe is the largest database of bereaved African American students yet assembled and examined distinctive features of their grief (Laurie and Neimeyer, forthcoming).

More than 1,600 bereaved college students, nearly 650 of whom were African American, participated in the study. Respondents completed the meaning-oriented and continuing-connections measures described earlier, as well as questions regarding the circumstances surrounding their losses. Results indicated that African American students experienced more frequent bereavement by homicide (11 percent) than their white peers (2 percent) but lower levels of suicide and accidents. African American participants—in contrast to their white peers—also described higher levels of grief, stronger continuing connections with the deceased, greater distress over the loss of kin beyond the immediate family, and a stronger sense of support in their grief, although they were less likely to talk with others about the loss or seek professional support for it.

Among the implications of these results for bereavement support for African American students are that educators and counselors should perhaps expect that grief may be more acute for these students than they assert; in other words, a norm of "being strong through suffering" could lead some bereaved blacks to minimize their distress. A second factor to consider is the tendency of African American students to experience more grief for the loss of extended relationships beyond the nuclear family as a function of the supportive system of kinship that reaches beyond parents and siblings to include relationships with grandparents, aunts, uncles, cousins, friends, and members of the church community. From the standpoint of intervention, this implies not only that educators and counselors should respect the emotional significance of losses of seemingly "distant" kin, but they also might seek to use such expanded systems in supporting bereaved students. They might, for example, conduct grief support within the campus religious community, black student groups, and other relevant organizations. The more frequent occurrence of homicide bereavement among African American students suggests the importance of tailoring interventions for this population, such as by drawing on the narrative and support group structures now being developed for groups affected by this tragic form of loss (Rynearson, 2006). As this research suggests, more attention should be given to the distinctive needs and resources of communities defined not only by ethnicity but also by sex, sex-role orientation, and other relevant dimensions.

Practical Points to Remember and Apply

Bereavement may be a silent epidemic on campuses. Although most students cope with death losses effectively, others experience protracted and debilitating symptoms. Campus professionals must be sensitive to the prevalence of grief on campuses and consider the implications as they interact with students, develop programs, and determine policy.

Many students troubled by grief may present counselors, academic advisers, faculty members, or other campus professionals with problems that are secondary to the loss, such as impaired ability to concentrate on their studies and reliance on alcohol or drugs. Insomnia, especially the kind that worsens over the first few months following loss, can be an important marker of complication and a focus for intervention. Campus professionals must be attuned to the behaviors that can indicate an internal struggle with bereavement and assess and intervene appropriately (including referring the student for mental health–related services).

Although all deaths can be challenging for bereaved students to integrate into their life stories, those arising from violent circumstances may be the hardest. Joining students in a quest to make sense of such losses is important, although counselors and educators should avoid offering easy answers to difficult questions. Efforts can be designed to assist students in the face of violent death losses; depending on the campus context, these efforts could be individual or institutionwide.

Finding some silver lining in the dark cloud of loss, such as affirming movement toward greater compassion, growth, and maturity, can be helpful to bereaved students. Counselors and others should not push students toward insights for which they are not ready, nor should anyone imply that they should let go of their pain and "look on the bright side." When meeting with bereaved students on an individual basis, educators should be open to comments about benefit-finding while avoiding minimizing the student's experience of loss.

For many students, maintaining a connection with their loved one beyond death (through such means as cultivating memories, recording or sharing stories, or continuing the person's legacy in the student's own life) can be a constructive response to loss. Counselors should be aware, however, that a close connection in the absence of a sense of meaning in the loss can be associated with more, rather than less, distress. Therefore, counselors should be attuned to bereaved students who display evidence of connection while also being able to find little or no meaning in the loss. Students grieve differently as a function of who they are; there is no single "normal" way to adapt to the loss of a significant person in one's life. Cultural and ethnic differences in experiences of death and practices related to death should be understood and respected and should be reflected in responses to the bereaved. Colleges and universities must therefore attend to both the unique needs and unique strengths of various groups in the services they provide and the outreach they offer.

Conclusion

Bereavement is among the most stressful life experiences and transitions experienced by college students, not only because of its prevalence but also because it can negatively affect developmental tasks associated with traditional-age students. Nevertheless, if integrated meaningfully into a student's life story, loss can foster personal growth. Consider the following words from Patricia, the student whose father had a heart attack while helping her move into her residence hall, expressed as she was about to graduate:

> Overall, I try to live life fully now, and I am less ruled by fear. I think I take more risks in relationships and try to keep from just hiding behind my accomplishments. I do not want necessarily to be remembered for what I did but more for who I am.
>
> I have a greater understanding of the humanness of all people. I think that before, I might have not really understood how there is no "superhuman" person who can move through life forever. We are all affected by our human condition. Everyone has loss, and everyone dies. I think that awareness brings me into a more open stance with getting to know and connect with others . . . . Maybe my father taught me that love does not have to be an action. Love is a presence, a knowing, and a way of being.

We hope that our research makes a small contribution to such life-affirming outcomes, pointing not only to the possible pitfalls of bereavement but also to possibilities for growth as students negotiate the transition from mourning to meaning.

References

Attig, T. *How We Grieve: Relearning the World.* New York: Oxford University Press, 1996.

Balk, D. E. "Death, Bereavement, and College Students: A Descriptive Analysis." *Mortality*, 1997, 2, 207–220.

Balk, D. E. "College Student Bereavement, Scholarship, and the University." *Death Studies,* 2001, *25,* 67–84.

Bonanno, G. A. "Loss, Trauma, and Human Resilience." *American Psychologist,* 2004, *59,* 20–28.

Calhoun, L., and Tedeschi, R. G. (eds.). *Handbook of Posttraumatic Growth.* Mahwah, N.J.: Erlbaum, 2006.

Chickering, A. W., and L. Reisser. "The Seven Vectors." In K. Arnold and I. C. King (eds.), *College Student Development and Academic Life.* New York: Garland, 1997.

Currier, J., Holland, J., Coleman, R., and Neimeyer, R. A. "Bereavement Following Violent Death: An Assault on Life and Meaning." In R. Stevenson and G. Cox (eds.), *Perspectives on Violence and Violent Death.* Amityville, N.Y.: Baywood, 2006.

Currier, J., Holland, J., and Neimeyer, R. A. "Sense-Making, Grief, and the Experience of Violent Loss: Toward a Mediational Model." *Death Studies,* 2006, *30,* 403–428.

Davis, C. G., Nolen-Hoeksema, S., and Larson, J. "Making Sense of Loss and Benefiting from the Experience: Two Construals of Meaning." *Journal of Personality and Social Psychology,* 1998, *75,* 561–574.

Edmonds, S., and Hooker, K. "Perceived Changes in Life Meaning Following Bereavement." *Omega,* 1992, *25,* 307–318.

Gillies, J., and Neimeyer, R. A. "Loss, Grief, and the Search for Significance: Toward a Model of Meaning Reconstruction in Bereavement." *Journal of Constructivist Psychology,* 2006, *19,* 31–65.

Hardison, H. G., Neimeyer, R. A., and Lichstein, K. L. "Insomnia and Complicated Grief Symptoms in Bereaved College Students." *Behavioral Sleep Medicine,* 2005, *3,* 99–111.

Hedtke, L., and Winslade, J. *Remembering Conversations.* Amityville, N.Y.: Baywood, 2003.

Holland, J., Currier, J., and Neimeyer, R. A. "Meaning Reconstruction in the First Two Years of Bereavement: The Role of Sense-Making and Benefit-Finding." *Omega,* 2006, *53,* 175–191.

Janoff-Bulman, R. "Assumptive Worlds and the Stress of Traumatic Events." *Social Cognition,* 1989, *7,* 113–116.

Janowiak, S. M., Mei-Tal, R., and Drapkin, R. G. "Living with Loss: A Group for Bereaved College Students." *Death Studies,* 1995, *19,* 55–63.

Kelly, G. A. *The Psychology of Personal Constructs.* New York: Norton, 1955.

Klass, D., Silverman, P. R., and Nickman, S. *Continuing Bonds: New Understandings of Grief.* Philadelphia: Taylor & Francis, 1996.

Laurie, A., and Neimeyer, R. A. "African Americans and Bereavement: Grief as a Function of Ethnicity." *Omega,* forthcoming.

Lichstein, K. L. "Behavioral Assessment and Treatment of Insomnia: A Review with an Emphasis on Clinical Application." *Behavior Therapy,* 1994, *25,* 659–688.

Neimeyer, R. A. *Lessons of Loss: A Guide to Coping.* (2nd ed.). New York: Brunner-Routledge, 2002.

Neimeyer, R. A. "Fostering Posttraumatic Growth: A Narrative Contribution." *Psychological Inquiry,* 2004, *15,* 53–59.

Neimeyer, R. A. "Widowhood, Grief, and the Quest for Meaning: A Narrative Perspective on Resilience." In D. Carr, R. M. Nesse, and C. B. Wortman (eds.), *Late Life Widowhood in the United States.* New York: Springer, 2006.

Neimeyer, R. A., and Anderson, A. "Meaning Reconstruction Theory." In N. Thompson (ed.), *Loss and Grief: A Guide for Human Service Practitioners.* New York: Palgrave Macmillan, 2002.

Neimeyer, R. A., Baldwin, S. A., and Gillies, J. "Continuing Bonds and Reconstructing Meaning: Mitigating Complications in Bereavement." *Death Studies,* 2006, *30,* 715–738.

Neimeyer, R. A., and Mahoney, M. J. *Constructivism in Psychotherapy.* Washington, D.C.: American Psychological Association, 1995.

Ott, C. H. "The Impact of Complicated Grief on Mental and Physical Health at Various Points in the Bereavement Process." *Death Studies*, 2003, *27*, 249–272.

Prigerson, H. G., and Maciejewski, P. K. "A Call for Sound Empirical Testing and Evaluation of Criteria for Complicated Grief Proposed by the DSM-V." *Omega*, 2006, *52*, 9–19.

Rosenblatt, P. C., and Wallace, B. R. "Narratives of Grieving African-Americans about Racism in the Lives of Deceased Family Members." *Death Studies*, 2005, *29*, 217–235.

Rynearson, E. K. (ed.). *Violent Death: Resilience and Intervention Beyond the Crisis.* New York: Routledge, 2006.

Schultz, L. "The Influence of Maternal Loss on Young Women's Experience of Identity Development in Emerging Adulthood." *Death Studies*, 2007, *31*, 17–43.

Shear, K., Frank, E., Houch, P. R., and Reynolds, C. F. "Treatment of Complicated Grief: A Randomized Controlled Trial." *Journal of the American Medical Association*, 2005, *293*, 2601–2608.

Zhang, B., El-Jawahri, A., and Prigerson, H. G. "Update on Bereavement Research: Evidence-Based Guidelines for the Diagnosis and Treatment of Complicated Bereavement." *Journal of Palliative Care*, 2006, *9*, 1188–1203.

ROBERT A. NEIMEYER *is professor of psychology at the University of Memphis.*

ANNA LAURIE, TARA MEHTA, *and* JOSEPH M. CURRIER *are doctoral students in clinical psychology at the University of Memphis.*

HEATHER HARDISON *is a psychologist in private practice in Tennessee.*

4

This chapter offers practical guidelines for conducting grief workshops on college campuses.

Designing and Conducting Grief Workshops for College Students

Craig J. Vickio

If colleges and universities are truly committed to promoting the well-being of their students and fostering their academic success, they must attend to the needs of grieving students (Balk, 2001). One way to do this is to invite students to use the university's counseling services following the death of a loved one. However, although grief counseling can be of benefit to bereaved students, many students might not perceive their grief as a mental health issue (Balk, 2001) and might therefore be disinclined to seek counseling.

As an alternative to counseling, some bereaved students might benefit from participating in structured grief support groups (Balk, Tyson-Rawson, and Colletti-Wetzel, 1993; Janowiak, Mei-Tal, and Drapkin, 1995). Such groups can, however, require a substantial commitment of time from group leaders as well as members; furthermore, some students might feel stigmatized by participating in a support group.

The purpose of this chapter is to propose a third alternative for assisting bereaved college students: psychoeducational workshops. Psychoeducational workshops are relatively unlikely to evoke student concerns regarding stigmatization, since workshops are offered in college settings so frequently. Whereas traditional mental health interventions are aimed at providing therapeutic treatment, psychoeducational workshops tend to be more didactic in their focus. Grief workshops emphasize informational resources and can be facilitated by counseling staff or other trained campus professionals. Also, unlike therapy, such workshops generally require limited staff time, do not entail establishing a confidential and ongoing

NEW DIRECTIONS FOR STUDENT SERVICES, no. 121, Spring 2008 © Wiley Periodicals, Inc.
Published online in Wiley InterScience (www.interscience.wiley.com) • DOI: 10.1002/ss.265

relationship with clients, and do not involve the creation of clinical records. Grief workshops of this sort can serve many important functions, including the following:

- Providing students with a conceptual framework for understanding their loss
- Normalizing and legitimizing students' grief-related thoughts and feelings
- Enabling students to interact with other bereaved individuals and thereby feel less isolated by their grief experience
- Helping students identify options for coping with their grief
- Directing students to other resources

This chapter furnishes campus professionals with practical guidelines for conducting grief workshops. After addressing how to plan a grief workshop, I present an overview of potential risks associated with conducting grief workshops and cite key recommendations for mitigating such risks and enhancing a workshop's utility. The chapter concludes with a discussion of content areas that might be covered in a grief workshop.

Planning a Grief Workshop for College Students

Preparing to offer a psychoeducational grief workshop (or a series of workshops) is in some respects a simpler process than offering more traditional mental health services such as individual or group counseling. Because the goal of a workshop is to provide education and support rather than treatment, such a program requires no advance screening of participants and allows for greater flexibility in facilitator credentials. Nevertheless, careful planning is essential to help ensure a workshop's success. Among the issues that must be addressed are the following five.

1. *What process should be used in determining goals and selecting content for the workshop?* Choices regarding workshop content should be guided by a consideration of the nature of the individual campus and an assessment of the participants' needs. If a campus has experienced a recent and prominent death, a workshop might be developed to address the needs of students affected by that loss.

The needs of individual participants can and should be assessed at the start of the workshop. Therefore, facilitators would be well advised to prepare a variety of materials for possible inclusion in their presentation. Such preparation will enable facilitators to tailor their program to the students who choose to attend. For instance, students grappling with diverging, incongruent grief-related feelings might profit from hearing about the paradoxical nature of grief experiences. For students who are unfamiliar with the grief process, a conceptual framework to help them make sense of their experience (for example, discussing common tasks associated with grief in contrast to the idea of linear stages of grief) might be useful. Students who have experienced losses of a traumatic nature can profit from learning ways that trauma can both hinder and facilitate grieving. Finally, students who have worked through various aspects of their grief might benefit from opportunities to explore ways to grow through their grief and move forward with their lives (Oltjenbruns, 1991). More detailed information about all of these topics is offered following the discussion of potential risks.

2. *How should the workshop be structured?* A psychoeducational grief workshop should include, at the least, an initial didactic component (a presentation about grief, for example) and time for participants to share experiences and concerns. By including time for sharing, the workshop can function in part as an opportunity for support. Plan on at least ninety minutes to ensure sufficient time for both components.

3. *Who should facilitate the workshop?* In identifying who should facilitate a grief workshop, the following issues should be considered:

- Identify facilitators who are both knowledgeable about grief and effective at establishing connections with students. It might be advantageous for one of the facilitators to be trained as a counselor, but this is not necessary. Potential facilitators can gain additional knowledge and training about grief by attending conferences and reading appropriate texts, such as those offered by the Association for Death Education and Counseling and Compassion Books.
- Be conscious of the possibility that talking with students about their grief experiences will evoke emotional reactions in your facilitators (Balk, Tyson-Rawson, and Colletti-Wetzel, 1993). Whenever possible, refrain from using facilitators who have experienced recent major losses in their own lives.
- Consider using two facilitators. This allows one facilitator to focus on the overall group process while the other attends to the reactions of individual participants (Vickio and Clark, 1998).

4. *Where and when should the workshop be held?* In making arrangements to hold a workshop, seek a location that is accessible to students yet also affords them a quiet, private, and comfortable space. Schedule the workshop at a time that is most convenient to students, such as during the dinner hour or following the conclusion of evening classes. If the workshop facilitators are aware of a particular group of students affected by a recent loss, the facilitators might attempt to schedule the workshop at a time particularly convenient for those students.

5. *How should the workshop be publicized?* Facilitators should consider how students on their campuses are mostly likely to hear about workshops and take advantage of such means of communication. Counseling center staff and other student affairs professionals might distribute flyers describing the upcoming workshop. The workshop can also be promoted by purchasing advertisements in the campus newspaper or by encouraging the newspaper's journalists to write a feature story on grief. Efforts also can be

made to advertise the workshop by including the program in calendars publicizing campuswide events and by sending information via university electronic mailing lists.

Grief Workshops: Potential Risks

Although grief workshops can be beneficial, they can also pose risks. Whenever counselors or student affairs professionals conduct a grief workshop, they face the potential for exacerbating the emotional reactions of some of the participants or rekindling reactions associated with past grief-related experiences. Also, in attempting to address the needs of the entire audience, facilitators may fail to attend to important differences among participants sufficiently.

Furthermore, the didactic segment of the workshop may be perceived by some participants as affording a neatly packaged intellectualized model that fails to capture the affective, phenomenological experience of their grief. When attempting to engender feelings of hopefulness or when addressing opportunities to grow through grief, facilitators can run the risk of being perceived as minimizing the painful aspects associated with loss. Although such potential risks are quite real, there are ways to minimize them or their impact.

Minimizing Risks and Enhancing the Effectiveness of Grief Workshops

When conducting grief workshops, several steps can be taken to reduce the risks I have outlined and to heighten the overall effectiveness of the workshop.

1. *Recognize and address diversity.* Facilitators must acknowledge the many differences that exist among members of the audience. Workshop participants are likely to demonstrate considerable diversity in the types of losses they have faced. They are also likely to differ in many other important respects, including personalities, developmental issues, age groups, coping styles, faith traditions, cultural heritages, and past experiences with loss. Even when participants appear to have much in common (such as two sophomores whose siblings have died), facilitators should avoid the temptation to gloss over their differences. These students might find some solace in giving voice to the shared aspects of their experience, but their grief and grieving are likely to differ in important ways. Workshop facilitators can help students recognize the uniqueness of their grief reactions by discussing diversity issues in the didactic portion of their program; facilitators can also highlight participants' different grief experiences as they emerge during the open discussion period.

2. *Invite participants to share their thoughts and experiences, but do not force disclosure.* Many workshop participants may find the time devoted to mutual sharing valuable. Such sharing allows participants to feel heard and understood in a caring environment. But participants should be afforded personal control, and facilitators should respect their right to keep certain

NEW DIRECTIONS FOR STUDENT SERVICES • DOI: 10.1002/ss

thoughts and feelings private. For example, addressing questions to the group as a whole is preferable to asking students to go around the circle with the expectation that all will speak. Some participants who elect to share little out loud may nevertheless profit immensely from having attended the program.

3. *Be aware that workshop content can elicit strong emotional reactions from participants.* In the introductory segment of the workshop, explain that parts of the ensuing discussion might evoke strong emotional reactions. If participants feel distressed during the program, invite them to take appropriate steps to attend to their personal needs. For example, facilitators can suggest that they "tune out" for a brief time or even remove themselves from the setting temporarily. If two facilitators are present, one could step out and talk with students who depart abruptly. Students who experience strong reactions to the program may benefit from an opportunity for individual conversations with the facilitators after the workshop. Such conversation could lead to a referral for treatment if warranted (for example, if the student reports a sense of isolation, speaks of substance abuse, or admits to thoughts of suicide or self-harm).

4. *Avoid overly intellectualized descriptions of grief.* Strive to share (and to elicit) personal stories that illustrate key points appropriately. Recounting true stories of others' grief experiences can be quite moving; sharing such stories can provide vivid illustrations of how others have dealt with their grief and found effective coping strategies. Such personal examples can shift the workshop from an academic lecture to an experiential event and thereby help facilitators reach participants at a much deeper level.

Workshop Topics

This section contains suggestions for content in psychoeducational grief workshops. These suggestions are intended as an outline of key ideas to be addressed, not a verbatim script for presentation. Prospective facilitators must tailor the specific details of their presentation to the needs of their audiences.

The Polarities of Grief. Bereaved students may feel pulled in multiple and conflicting directions. For example, they may find themselves alternating between the need to face their loss and the desire to avoid confronting it. Workshop participants can benefit from hearing that such conflicting feelings are normal and that important functions are served both by confronting and by avoiding their loss. By facing their loss, the bereaved can find opportunities for coming to terms with reality and for relearning their world. By avoiding thoughts of death and loss, the bereaved are given a respite from the painful, difficult work of grieving and can attend to other aspects of their lives (Neimeyer, 2000; Stroebe and Schut, 1999).

The process of grieving can entail wrestling with other polarities, including such quandaries as these:

Should I hold on to my relationship with the deceased or let go?
Is this loss simply a reminder that my life is ultimately meaningless, or am I being given the chance to discover a deeper meaning to life?
Is grief a passive process that I must undergo, or can I make conscious choices about the ways that I grieve?

Discussing such polarities can help workshop participants recognize that there are no clear-cut answers. Participants can be helped to recognize that grieving is a very complex process that entails both holding on and letting go, confronting and avoiding, conflicting perceptions regarding life's meaning, and experiencing loss passively while making active decisions about how to handle it. The challenge for the bereaved is to integrate such polarities by honoring *both* sides of these seemingly opposing forces and recognizing the legitimacy of each.

The Tasks of Grief. Didactic information about the key tasks associated with grief can provide workshop participants with a conceptual model or framework for attributing meaning to their experiences. Presenting a task model of grief (in which the grief process is framed as a series of tasks) rather than a stage model (in which grief is conceptualized as involving a succession of stages) has a couple of advantages. First, students are likely to feel more empowered by conceptualizing their grief as entailing a series of tasks they can undertake rather than a series of stages that they will experience passively. Second, unlike stage models of grief, the task model is more flexible: it assumes no rigid, preordained order in which grief tasks must be undertaken. In fact, the tasks may be addressed simultaneously rather than in sequence.

Four tasks are commonly associated with grieving: (1) accepting the reality of the death, (2) doing one's duty to the deceased, (3) reestablishing a sense of control, and (4) revising one's worldview (Attig, 1996, 2000; Neimeyer, 2000; Rando, 1993; Worden, 1991). As facilitators explain the grief tasks, they must consider the developmental levels of participants (see Chapter Two). Because, for example, many college students of traditional age are likely to be dualistic in their thinking (Perry, 1968), workshop facilitators should emphasize the fact that there is no single right way to accomplish any particular grief task.

1. *Accepting the reality of the death.* Facilitators should acknowledge and also ask participants about the challenges of accepting that a loved one has died. As bereaved college students struggle to accept this reality, they may find themselves searching their environment for the person who has died, sensing the presence of the deceased, or engaging in an obsessive review of the deceased's life or death (Vickio and Clark, 1998). Students can be reassured to hear that such actions are common and serve an important purpose: helping the bereaved come to terms with the harsh reality that a loved one has died.

In further commenting on the challenge of accepting the reality of one's loss, workshop facilitators may choose to raise other related points for discussion. They may, for example, state that accepting a loss is an ongoing

NEW DIRECTIONS FOR STUDENT SERVICES • DOI: 10.1002/ss

process rather than a onetime event. Even after acknowledging that a loved one has died, the bereaved may still have difficulty accepting this reality on an emotional level or may be unaware of the attendant or "secondary" losses that can accompany the physical absence of the loved one. For college students, key secondary losses may include the dashing of future opportunities, such as having the deceased present at their college graduation ceremony or other major life events, as well as the loss of certain fundamental beliefs about the world. Bereaved students can benefit from knowing that their struggles are normal and that with time, they can expect to accommodate to the many ways that their loss will affect their lives.

2. *Doing one's duty to the deceased.* Participants can benefit from learning that it is typical for many bereaved individuals to seek to honor the deceased and to feel regret or guilt for not doing so while the loved one was alive. Facilitators should help participants recognize that such feelings are normal and explore means to honor the deceased. This exploration can include acknowledging that doing one's duty to the deceased can take forms that are adaptive or maladaptive. For instance, feeling the need to suffer in honor of the deceased can be unhealthy for the survivor. In contrast, striving to build on the deceased's legacy can imbue survivors' lives with a heightened sense of purposefulness. This is particularly true when individuals balance duty to honor the deceased with duty to be true to themselves (Vickio, 1999). Although offering this information can be useful, facilitators are likely to have a greater impact by encouraging participants to share thoughts and ideas with one another (Yalom, 1995).

3. *Regaining a sense of personal control.* Following the death of a loved one, the bereaved might experience a pronounced sense of helplessness (Parkes, 1991; Rynearson, Johnson, and Correa, 2006). Workshop facilitators should acknowledge this sense of helplessness and note that bereaved students may struggle to accept that they lack control over many of their life circumstances. Facilitators might also note that this challenge can be especially troubling for grieving college students, many of whom are wrestling with the developmental task of establishing autonomy (Balk, 2001).

Facilitators can, however, also help participants realize the extent to which they *can* make important life choices. Grieving is an active process that affords individuals a wide array of options for coping (Attig, 1996, 2000; Neimeyer, 1997). Through the process of making active choices about how to perceive and respond to loss, the bereaved can experience a renewed sense of meaning and purpose. Facilitators can promote discussion focused on the topic of choices and encourage members to share personal methods of coping.

4. *Making sense of the world.* Experiencing the death of a loved one can violate certain core beliefs about life (Attig, 1996; Rando, 1993; Vickio, 2000), but it also provide opportunities to construct new belief systems that are compatible with the experience of death. Furthermore, facing the death of a loved one can prompt development of new perspectives on the world that focus attention on what truly matters and promote living life more fully

NEW DIRECTIONS FOR STUDENT SERVICES • DOI: 10.1002/ss

(Attig, 1996, 2000; Braun and Berg, 1994; Janoff-Bulman, 1992; Milo, 1997; Neimeyer, 1997, 2000; Oltjenbruns, 1991; Weenolsen, 1996). In grief workshops, facilitators can assist participants in considering such a perspective. Students can be encouraged to think about how their lives have changed and how their worldviews have shifted in the aftermath of loss. Making sense of the world following a death can, for example, entail recognizing the preciousness of each moment and the importance of connections with others.

Intersection Between Trauma and Grief. Students who have faced losses of a sudden and violent nature are likely to experience reactions that are both similar to and distinct from normal grief reactions (Bonanno and Kaltman, 2001; Neimeyer, Prigerson, and Davies, 2002; Regehr and Sussman, 2004). Traumatized students who are also grieving can benefit from understanding such similarities and differences because this information can have important implications for how they cope with their loss. Note that although grief and trauma (for example, emotional pain, distress, and shock following an extreme event) are experiences that often overlap, they are distinct concepts. Individuals may experience a death that is or is not traumatic just as they can experience trauma that does or does not involve death.

Like grief, the experience of trauma can include shock, numbness, and disbelief; difficulty acknowledging the reality of what has occurred; alternating between confrontation and avoidance of stimuli; violation of fundamental beliefs; and irritability and anger. Beyond these similarities, trauma has unique symptoms that can hinder the bereaved by interfering with the cognitive processing that grief work requires (Neimeyer, Prigerson, and Davies, 2002). Trauma symptoms include heightened physiological reactivity; a pronounced sense of endangerment; hypervigilance; fragmented, intrusive images; and dissociation (American Psychiatric Association, 2000).

To be free to work on the tasks associated with grief, bereaved individuals may need treatment for their trauma symptoms. Possible treatments for trauma include therapeutic use of grounding strategies, anxiety management techniques, relaxation training, systematic desensitization, cognitive restructuring, distraction and refocusing strategies, mindfulness techniques, and medication.

Growing Through Grief. Students who have moved beyond the initial shock of their loss and have made progress in coming to terms with accepting its reality may benefit from an extended discussion of positive facets of grief experience. By discussing opportunities to grow through grief, workshop facilitators can encourage their participants to develop a sense of hopefulness about their future lives. In elaborating on this task, facilitators could present different approaches to maintaining meaningful, rewarding connections with the person who has died (Attig, 2000; Vickio, 1999). Workshop discussion also can include an in-depth examination of new worldviews that can be forged in the aftermath of loss, such as the view that life is a gift rather than a right.

NEW DIRECTIONS FOR STUDENT SERVICES • DOI: 10.1002/ss

Additional Comments About Topic Selection

The list of topics cited so far is by no means exhaustive, and there is considerable overlap among them. All of the topics entail altering one's fundamental beliefs about life and, to some degree, changing the ways that one relates to the world (Attig, 1996; Neimeyer, 2000). Given the significant links that exist among the topics, workshop facilitators may wish to incorporate discussion of a variety of interrelated issues (such as doing one's duty and finding meaning) into their programs.

As facilitators interact with bereaved students and learn their specific needs, facilitators may discover that participants would profit from information beyond what I have outlined in this chapter. Students may wish to learn more about subjects such as grief and spirituality, gender differences in grief, similarities and differences between grief and depression, emotions associated with grief, and ways to help others who are grieving.

Conclusion

Many college students must contend with the death of a friend or loved one. Students' grief experiences have the potential to disrupt all facets of their lives significantly. Although grieving students differ tremendously in their coping skills and overall levels of resilience, many are apt to benefit from participating in educational workshops on grief and loss. Such workshops can help students make sense of their grief, feel validated in their experiences, identify options for coping, and derive needed support from their peers.

References

American Psychiatric Association. *Diagnostic and Statistical Manual of Mental Disorders.* (4th ed., text rev.). Washington, D.C.: American Psychiatric Association, 2000.

Attig, T. *How We Grieve: Relearning the World.* New York: Oxford University Press, 1996.

Attig, T. *The Heart of Grief: Death and the Search for Lasting Love.* New York: Oxford University Press, 2000.

Balk, D. E. "College Student Bereavement, Scholarship, and the University: A Call for University Engagement." *Death Studies,* 2001, 25, 67–84.

Balk, D. E., Tyson-Rawson, K., and Colletti-Wetzel, J. "Social Support as an Intervention with Bereaved College Students." *Death Studies,* 1993, 17, 427–450.

Bonanno, G. A., and Kaltman, S. "The Varieties of Grief Experience." *Clinical Psychology Review,* 2001, 21, 705–734.

Braun, M. J., and Berg, D. H. "Meaning Reconstruction in the Experience of Parental Bereavement." *Death Studies,* 1994, 18, 105–129.

Janoff-Bulman, R. *Shattered Assumptions: Towards a New Psychology of Trauma.* New York: Free Press, 1992.

Janowiak, S. M., Mei-Tal, R., and Drapkin, R. G. "Living with Loss: A Group for Bereaved College Students." *Death Studies,* 1995, 19, 55–63.

Milo, E. M. "Maternal Responses to the Life and Death of a Child with a Developmental Disability: A Story of Hope." *Death Studies,* 1997, 21, 443–476.

Neimeyer, R. A. "Meaning Reconstruction and the Experience of Chronic Loss." In K. J. Doka (ed.), *Living with Grief: When Illness Is Prolonged.* Philadelphia: Taylor & Francis, 1997.

Neimeyer, R. A. *Lessons of Loss: A Guide to Coping.* Keystone Heights, Fla.: PsychoEducational Resources, 2000.

Neimeyer, R. A., Prigerson, H. G., and Davies, B. "Mourning and Meaning." *American Behavioral Scientist,* 2002, *46,* 235–251.

Oltjenbruns, K. A. "Positive Outcomes of Adolescents' Experience with Grief." *Journal of Adolescent Research,* 1991, *6,* 43–53.

Parkes, C. M. "Attachment, Bonding, and Psychiatric Problems After Bereavement in Adult Life." In C. M. Murray, J. Stevenson-Hinde, and P. Marris (eds.), *Attachment Across the Lifespan.* New York: Tavistock-Routledge, 1991.

Perry, W. G., Jr. *Forms of Intellectual and Ethical Development in the College Years: A Scheme.* Austin, Tex.: Holt, Rinehart and Winston, 1968.

Rando, T. A. *Treatment of Complicated Mourning.* Champaign, Ill.: Research Press, 1993.

Regehr, C., and Sussman, T. "Intersections Between Grief and Trauma: Toward an Empirically Based Model for Treating Traumatic Grief." *Brief Treatment and Crisis Intervention,* 2004, *4,* 289–309.

Rynearson, E. K., Johnson, T. A., and Correa, F. "The Horror and Helplessness of Violent Death." In R. S. Katz and T. A. Johnson (eds.), *When Professionals Weep: Emotional and Countertransference Responses in End-of-Life Care.* New York: Routledge, 2006.

Stroebe, M. S., and Schut, H. "The Dual Process Model of Coping with Bereavement: Rationale and Description." *Death Studies,* 1999, *23,* 197–224.

Vickio, C. J. "Together in Spirit: Keeping Our Relationships Alive When Loved Ones Die." *Death Studies,* 1999, *23,* 161–175.

Vickio, C. J. "Developing Beliefs That Are Compatible with Death: Revising Our Assumptions About Predictability, Control, and Continuity." *Death Studies,* 2000, *24,* 739–758.

Vickio, C. J., and Clark, C. A. "Growing Through Grief: A Psychoeducational Workshop Series for Bereaved Students." *Journal of College Student Development,* 1998, *39,* 621–623.

Weenolsen, P. *The Art of Dying.* New York: St. Martin's Press, 1996.

Worden, W. *Grief Counseling and Grief Therapy: A Handbook for the Mental Health Practitioner.* (2nd ed.). New York: Springer, 1991.

Yalom, I. D. *The Theory and Practice of Group Psychotherapy.* New York: Basic Books, 1995.

CRAIG J. VICKIO *is a clinical psychologist and director of the counseling center at Bowling Green State University in Ohio.*

5

The authors provide guidance for conducting workshops on bereavement for faculty members and resident assistants who, because of their regular interactions with students, are well positioned to respond to students in difficulty.

Training Faculty Members and Resident Assistants to Respond to Bereaved Students

Heather L. Servaty-Seib, Deborah J. Taub

Scholarship about campus responses to death-related events emphasizes the need for members of the campus community to be open to discussing grief-related issues (Rickgarn, 1996; Steufert, 2004). Faculty members and resident assistants (RAs) are ideally situated to observe and respond to bereaved students. Faculty—tenure-track, adjunct, and teaching assistants—have regular contact with students and can detect the negative effects of bereavement on academic performance at the earliest point (Servaty-Seib and Hamilton, 2006). They can also be the most consistent points of contact with the institution for commuter students (Jacoby, 1989). Resident assistants interact with resident students in their on-campus homes and are most likely to observe changes in functioning such as withdrawal, insomnia, and risky behaviors (Blimling, 2003).

Although these two groups are quite different, both have frequent contact with particular groups of students. Providing training to these two groups can help them respond to bereaved students effectively. This chapter provides guidance for workshops for faculty members and for RAs, with particular emphasis on how to reduce the experience of disenfranchised grief for bereaved students.

Content: Knowledge of Grief

A broad understanding of the normative, multidimensional, and unique nature and the general phases of grief helps in the support of bereaved students. In this section, we present a brief overview of the general knowledge that should underlie the training.

Grief is a normal process, a natural reaction to all types of losses (Rando, 1995). Although it can become problematic and interfere with general functioning in an extended and intense manner, in general, few grieving individuals develop severe or prolonged symptoms (Bonanno and Kaltman, 2001).

Although grief is often equated with sadness, it involves a range of responses, including physical, behavioral, emotional, social, cognitive, and spiritual symptoms. Research on the grief of college students suggests potential difficulties in all of these areas, including somatic complaints, insomnia, anger and bitterness, reduced trust, lowered personal life expectancy, decreased academic performance, and questions regarding faith in a higher power (Denes-Raj and Ehrlichman, 1991; Hardison, Neimeyer, and Lichstein, 2005; Servaty-Seib and Hamilton, 2006; Sklar and Hartley, 1990). College students may also experience growth in reaction to death losses, including increased ability to cope, increased emotional strength, increased empathy for others, better communication skills, and stronger emotional connections with others (Edmonds and Hooker, 1992; Oltjenbruns, 1991).

Grief is also unique to each person (Rando, 1995). Individuals grieve in their own way, based on who they are as people (whether they are introverted or extroverted, their degree of neuroticism, and so on) (Bonanno and others, 2002) and on their relationship with the person who died (Gilbert, 1989). Each grieving individual is likely to experience a distinct constellation of symptoms that can shift rapidly on a weekly, daily, and even hourly basis. This can be confusing to those who interact with bereaved individuals and to the bereaved individuals themselves.

As a process, grief does not lend itself well to the human desire for linear explanations for life processes. Students may interpret any stage theory of grief in a literal and prescriptive fashion. A preferable approach to conceptualizing grief—one that might lend itself less to the dangers of self-prescription—is a general phase approach. Most stage theories of grief have some similarities, including an initial period of shock and disbelief, a middle phase of acute pain signified by symptoms in all the areas noted earlier, and a final period characterized by a gradual improvement in symptoms and processes such as reintegration, transformation, and accommodation (DeSpelder and Strickland, 1996). As suggested by these phases, grief is not an acute response to a discrete event but rather a continuing development (Rando, 1995). Grieving individuals are not working to return to normal; they are working toward establishing a new normal. Bereaved individuals face the challenge of reorienting themselves to the loss itself (acknowledging and understanding the loss), the self (revising their sense of self and assumptions about the world), and the external world (learning to live in a healthy way now that their loved one is gone) (Attig, 1996; Neimeyer, 2001).

Disenfranchised grief is grief that is not generally acknowledged or recognized (Doka, 2002). An individual's grief might not be recognized because the relationship to the deceased is unknown to others (such as an undisclosed same-sex partner) or is deemed not close enough (such as the sibling of a person one is dating) or important enough (such as the death of a recently acquired friend or a miscarriage) to warrant grieving. Although the grief might be felt deeply by the individual, it is not confirmed or validated through interactions with others. Individuals experiencing disenfranchised grief are at risk for questioning the legitimacy of their own feelings and for intensified feelings of hopelessness, numbness, and guilt. Those whose grief is disenfranchised are likely to be isolated from potential supports and have few opportunities to express and process their grief.

Many aspects of campus environments can foster a sense of disenfranchised grief in bereaved college students. Among these aspects are a focus on academic achievement and performance, emphasis on independence and individualism, and a campus culture of fun and youth (Kadison and DiGeronimo, 2004; Nathan, 2005). It is not uncommon for bereaved students to struggle in the very areas that are often central to the college experience, particularly academics and interpersonal interactions (Meshot and Leitner, 1994; Servaty-Seib and Hamilton, 2006). Grieving students may serve as reminders to their peers (as well as to faculty and staff) of the frailty of life and the reality of death.

Research suggests that although traditional-age college students may understand some aspects of the bereaved experience, they may be less adept at offering appropriate support (Balk, 1997). Some traditional-age college students have not experienced death losses and may be less able than older adults to empathize with others. Peers (young and old alike) may have the expectation that bereaved students should "get over it" quickly and "get back to normal" so that they can rejoin activities and be a part of the group again (Silverman, 1987). Although their message may be one of wanting to reconnect with the bereaved individual, such responses minimize the extent of the bereaved person's experience and can foster disenfranchised grief. (See Chapter Two for an extended discussion of campus environments.)

Content: Skills and Strategies for Interacting with Bereaved Students

Because faculty members and RAs play critical, though different, roles in the lives of college students, they can engage in actions that will decrease the disenfranchised nature of students' grief: observing and questioning, taking time to listen, using statements that validate, offering tangible support, and referring when necessary. The purpose and impact of each of these actions can be presented and modeled in the training, and participants can practice each of them.

54 BEREAVED COLLEGE STUDENTS

Observe and Inquire. Faculty members can follow up with students whose academic performance has deteriorated (as evidenced by such things as a drop in grades or lack of attendance). Resident assistants can follow up on observations that students' social or behavioral functioning has deteriorated (manifested as withdrawal and isolation or increased alcohol use, for example). The action of following up (by seeking the student out to inquire if something is wrong, for instance) acknowledges that there are events outside of the academic arena that can and often do affect student functioning.

When following up with students about behavioral shifts, one must be as specific as possible about what has been observed and communicate a message of care and concern. Examples of appropriate statements include "I noticed that you have not been in class much the past few weeks. I just wanted you to know that I have noticed and that I am concerned about you" and "I haven't seen you around the floor much lately. Ben mentioned that your brother died. I can't imagine how tough that must be. Please let me know if there is anything I can do."

Sensitivity to death-related statements is also important. If a student makes a passing comment either in class or on the floor about needing to attend a funeral, the faculty member or the RA can comment, "I am sorry to hear that. Who was it who died? How close were you to that person . . . ? How hard it must be on you." Such statements and questions acknowledge the death loss experience immediately and directly and send the message that such experiences have real and meaningful effects on students' lives.

Take the Time to Listen. We would argue that the most powerful action one can engage in is taking time to listen to the experiences of bereaved students. Universities and colleges are busy places. The psychological benefit that a bereaved student will receive from someone's choice to take even ten or fifteen minutes to talk about his or her loss is difficult to overestimate. The act of taking this time, in and of itself, is a compelling counteraction to the disenfranchising messages that bereaved students may perceive. Faculty members can take such time during office hours or immediately after class, while RAs may have more flexibility to interact with bereaved students in the evenings and on the weekends.

Use Statements That Validate. Although nonbereaved individuals often struggle with what to say to the bereaved (James and Friedman, 1998), simply being present and communicating openness is more important than particular words. Bereaved individuals do not need a "magic bullet" statement (Burleson, 1998), intended to eliminate their grief; rather, they need messages that are person-centered (Burleson, 2003). Person-centeredness is the "extent to which a message validates, recognizes, and/or acknowledges the recipient's feelings and experiences" (Rack and others, forthcoming). Statements perceived by bereaved students as most helpful are messages high in person-centeredness, including "I am here for you," "I am a good listener if you need one," and "I really care about how you are doing." In contrast, the following messages are low in person-centeredness

NEW DIRECTIONS FOR STUDENT SERVICES • DOI: 10.1002/ss

and also are rated low in helpfulness by bereaved college students: "You shouldn't let this get you down," "Do not take it so hard," "You should keep busy," and "You must get on with your life" (Rack and others, forthcoming). Training should include the process of using messages high in person-centeredness. Because of the value faculty members place on evidence (Evenbeck and Jackson, 2005), the theoretical and empirical support for the use of such messages may be particularly compelling to faculty members.

Offer Tangible Support. Both faculty members and RAs are well situated to offer practical assistance to bereaved students. Grieving students' academic performance is negatively affected by the experience of bereavement, particularly during the semester of their death loss (Servaty-Seib and Hamilton, 2006). Faculty members may be in a position to offer more time for assignments and makeup exams and labs and to provide bereaved students with the opportunity to take "incompletes" in courses when appropriate. Such supports can make a tremendous difference for bereaved students who are in the acute stages of grief, struggling with symptoms such as concentration problems, insomnia, and somatic concerns.

As peers, RAs can offer assistance that is beyond the realm of those who have strictly professional roles on campus. They can knock on a bereaved student's door and ask about going to lunch or dinner or participating in an activity together. Resident assistants can keep attuned to student-related deadlines on campus (such as registration for classes, financial aid deadlines, and housing applications) and mention them casually in the presence of the bereaved student. Such deadlines might be missed by those who are bereaved, leading to serious adverse consequences such as loss of financial aid or of campus housing. In addition, RAs can contact campus counseling center professionals and arrange for programs focused on helping residents support one another during times of stress, including bereavement.

Refer as Necessary. Because of their frequent contact with students, faculty members and RAs should remain abreast of the support services available to students. For bereaved students, such services might include support groups or workshops, campus ministry programs, or campus-based memorial services. Faculty and RAs should be knowledgeable about relevant campus policies as well; they can serve students best by informing students of their rights and options. For example, bereaved students may not know if they can or cannot request an "incomplete" in a course in bereavement-related situations.

At times, bereaved students may need a direct message about counseling or even immediate mental health assistance if a crisis situation has developed. A referral for counseling is warranted if bereaved students' daily functioning is seriously and negatively affected, as when students become socially isolated, stop attending classes, gain or lose a significant amount of weight, engage in risky behavior such as increased drinking or sexual activity, or exhibit violent or aggressive tendencies. If bereaved students express suicidal thoughts or the idea that others would be better off if they were "not around," faculty members and RAs should offer to accompany them to the counseling center. Although it is common for bereaved individuals to want to be with the deceased loved one, comments that suggest a desire to die must be taken seriously and followed by action that leads to screening by a mental health professional.

Process: Practical Considerations and Structure

The processes to be used in delivering training for faculty members or RAs in working with bereaved students depend on the purposes and objectives of the workshop. What are the desired outcomes? What do the presenters want participants to take with them when they leave? These purposes and objectives might be thought about in terms of knowledge, skills, and dispositions and the workshop should address each of these.

Practical Considerations. Before addressing how these areas (knowledge, skills, and dispositions) can be addressed, however, there are many practical issues to consider, including who would lead these workshops, how long would they be, when and where would they be held, and how they should be promoted and advertised. We address each of these areas separately for faculty members and RAs, as the answers are distinct for each group.

For faculty members, workshops focused on bereaved students could be sponsored by the office that is responsible for faculty development, if such an office exists. Presenters and facilitators could be drawn from a number of different offices (depending on the structure of the particular institution), including the counseling center, the office of the dean of students, and campus ministries; perhaps there are faculty members for whom grief is a specialty. Collaboration among people who bring unique knowledge and expertise regarding the experience of bereaved students and the process of training faculty is optimal (Mosley, 1998).

The general literature on professional development for faculty often recommends daylong training sessions, and time frames such as $1\frac{1}{2}$ and 2 hours have been used when training faculty on interacting with "emotionally troubled" (Rodolfa, 1987) and angry (Cardozo, 1983) students. However, Godbey (1996) found that workshops that were kept to an hour or less and done over lunch were the best attended. With a specific topic such as grief, an hour is a good time frame for balancing both the time needed to cover the material and faculty availability. If the topic were broadened to address interacting with emotional students in general, a longer time frame of two hours would be required.

If the workshop were offered over lunch, it could be held in a separate room of one of the campus dining halls to facilitate purchasing of lunch by participants. The most critical issue to consider when choosing a location for such a workshop is proximity to faculty offices. Faculty are more likely to attend if the workshop is scheduled in a site that is convenient and easy to find.

Promoting the workshop is a crucial component of its success. General marketing practices suggest that individuals are more likely to remember and process information if they are exposed to the information at least three

NEW DIRECTIONS FOR STUDENT SERVICES • DOI: 10.1002/ss

times. Therefore, a variety of approaches to promotion are recommended, including flyers or letters sent to individual faculty and to deans and department heads, flyers posted on department bulletin boards, e-mail messages sent to department electronic mailing lists, statements for inclusion in campus newsletters, and a Web page with workshop information.

The practical issues regarding workshop logistics are quite different for RAs. Although the amount and type of training they receive vary, RAs are likely to have received mandatory training related to their roles and responsibilities (Twale and Muse, 1996). This training usually takes place in one of three forms: preservice training, in-service training, and training retreats; typically, a residential life system will employ more than one of these three formats (Bowman and Bowman, 1995). Often RA training is done in intensive sessions in the days or weeks immediately before their work begins, but it is sometimes done via credit-bearing courses far in advance of the start of their work (Bowman and Bowman, 1995). Issues of promotion, location, and marketing of the training are therefore not applicable to the RA audience.

In-service training to supplement preservice training is common in the education of RAs (Twale and Muse, 1996). An in-service training session could be a good format for providing RAs with information about responding to bereaved residents.

Recommended session length is the same for RAs as for faculty members. Potential presenters could be drawn from student-related offices, such as representatives from the office of the dean of students, academic advising, the student wellness office, the health center, campus ministries, and the counseling center. The use of such campus personnel is common in both preservice and in-service RA training (Twale and Muse, 1996). As with faculty training, collaboration can bring a variety of perspectives and facilitate interested parties across campus discussing grief-related issues.

Structure. We recommend an active, involved, and experiential approach to training for work with bereaved students. This approach is likely to hold participants' attention and therefore lead to greater retention (Weslowski, Bowman, and Adams, 1996). An experiential approach will address the areas of knowledge, skills, and dispositions most efficiently and effectively. In addition, a workshop that uses a variety of teaching methods is likely to respond to the preferred learning styles of all participants (Brooks-Harris and Stock-Ward, 1999). A common theme in the general literature focused on providing training to faculty members is the presentation of brief didactic information (knowledge) accompanied by experiential activities (skills and dispositions) such as role-plays, sharing of personal experiences, and small group discussions or activities (Brillant and Gribben, 1993; Cardozo, 1983; Rodolfa, 1987). Hands-on, experiential, and scenario- or situation-based training has been found to be popular with RAs (Twale and Muse, 1996). Practical training is more valued by RAs, especially new RAs, than more theoretical (ideas and concepts) training (Murray, Kagan, and Snider, 2001).

The specific nature of the experiential core of the workshop will differ, based on the unique environment and culture of each campus community. Differences exist with regard to participants' comfort in the level of personal sharing, the level of structure required for the use of role-plays (to be explained shortly), and the extent to which bereaved students can actually be involved in the training.

Members of some campus communities may be more open to sharing and working on personal examples, while others may feel more comfortable discussing hypothetical situations. Participants can be given the opportunity to share their experience of interacting with a bereaved student (see Brillant and Gribben, 1994; Rodolfa, 1987). These elements of sharing could be combined with small group and large group discussions, including feedback and ideas for fostering responses that could help reduce students' sense of disenfranchised grief. Similar discussion could take place after workshop participants have read or viewed vignettes portraying interactions between bereaved students and faculty or RAs. Rodolfa (1987) collaborated with the theater arts department to create such vignettes.

Role-playing is a powerful approach to building interpersonal skills and can be useful in training (Twale and Muse, 1996; Weslowski, Bowman, and Adams, 1996). In fact, faculty members rated the modeling and role-playing aspects of a workshop on dealing with angry students as the most useful aspects of the workshop (Cardozo, 1983). One should model appropriate responses prior to asking participants to attempt to role-play such responses. A highly structured approach to role-playing would include the use of scripts, which might illustrate both helpful and unhelpful responses or only unhelpful responses (see Mosley, 1998). Participants could be paired to read the scripts and discuss the differences in content, tone, and underlying goals of the approaches used in each script. A less structured approach would provide pairs of attendees with a general description of a bereavement-related situation, ask each member of the pair to write down how they would respond (see Cardozo, 1983), and ask them to enact the scenario once and then a second time, switching roles. All of these approaches could follow didactic information or could lead to the presentation of more specific content regarding the multidimensional nature of and myths about grief.

The extent to which bereaved students can or should be involved in a workshop focused on interacting with bereaved students depends on many factors, including the psychological openness of the student body, the level of student organization around grief and bereavement issues (more on this in a moment), and campus acknowledgment of grief and bereavement. A student body that is high in awareness of and openness to discussion of emotional issues is likely to include students who would be willing to discuss their own grief experiences. If a campus has an active support network for bereaved students, as is available through organizations such as the National Students of Ailing Mothers and Fathers Support Network, bereaved students might be easy to identify and invested in educating others about their experiences. If death issues are acknowledged and discussed openly on campus through campus memorial services, availability of support groups, and administrative communication regarding campus death losses, students are more likely to feel comfortable coming forward to talk about their experiences than if such openness does not exist.

Although involving bereaved students in the workshop might be complicated, such involvement is likely to be worth the effort. Hearing the stories of bereaved individuals in their own words can be powerful. A panel of bereaved students from whom participants could gain insight might be possible. A related approach is the use of videotaped or audiotaped statements from one or more bereaved students discussing some of their more difficult bereavement-related experiences on campus. Having participants read aloud statements written by bereaved students is another way to include the voices of bereaved individuals in the workshop.

Using electronic technologies as a means to provide training about working with bereaved students can also be useful. Institutions of higher education are using a variety of online approaches to provide faculty with training on topics such as the use of human subjects and maintaining a drug-free workplace. Online approaches to RA training, using course management software such as WebCT and Blackboard, are becoming more common (R. T. Hartwig, personal communication, April 27, 2007; T. M. Paczolt, personal communication, April 30, 2007). The use of podcasts to convey information is growing rapidly in higher education, due in part to the ubiquity of iPods and other MP3 players on campus, the ease of creating and distributing content, and the appeal of a portable format (Brown, 2006). Colleges and universities are exploring the possibility of using podcasts or other electronic approaches to provide suicide prevention training to faculty members and staff (M. Mannell, personal communication, March 6, 2007).

Although such approaches do not allow for direct contact among participants, there might be options for using experiential activities that could still result in skill building. For example, a Web-based program could begin with brief didactic information, transition into scenarios that offered both appropriate and less helpful responses, and end with an activity in which participants are presented with a segmented video of a bereaved student and asked to select from among various verbal responses at various points in the scenario. Participants could be provided with feedback regarding the extent of person-centeredness and helpfulness or unhelpfulness of each option. Although this format would require a large amount of programming and coordination, it could allow people to access the training in their own offices or homes, at times that are most convenient for them, and during times of particular need.

Extension of the Workshop to Other Members of the Campus Community

With some minor revisions, a workshop on bereaved students could be made available to other members of the campus community who have frequent contact with students. Potential audiences might include academic advisers, members of the student affairs staff, supervisors of student employees and work-study students, and campus service staff such as custodians and clerical and desk staff. In-service and luncheon formats might be particularly well suited to such audiences. The content of the workshop would be quite similar to that described earlier, with minor changes to recognize the different roles that these people play in students' lives. For example, offering tangible feedback to bereaved students could involve encouraging the use of vacation days by work-study supervisors, whereas academic advisers might offer to assist students in notifying faculty members about the death.

Conclusion

Bereavement is a common concern for college students (see Chapter One), and the grieving process has the potential to interfere with students' daily functioning and academic success. Faculty members and RAs have the potential to be helpful to bereaved students, but training focused on knowledge, skills, and dispositions is required. With such training, these individuals are in a powerful position to lessen the disenfranchised nature of bereaved students' experiences and assist them in adapting to their death losses.

References

Attig, T. *How We Grieve: Relearning the World.* New York: Oxford University Press, 1996.

Balk, D. E. "Death, Bereavement, and College Students: A Descriptive Analysis." *Mortality,* 1997, 2, 207–220.

Blimling, G. *The Resident Assistant.* (6th ed.). Dubuque, Iowa: Kendall/Hunt, 2003.

Bonanno, G. A., and Kaltman, S. "The Varieties of Grief Experience." *Clinical Psychology Review,* 2001, 21, 705–734.

Bonanno, G. A., and others. "Resilience to Loss and Chronic Grief: A Prospective Study from Preloss to 18-Months Postloss." *Journal of Personality and Social Psychology,* 2002, 83, 1150–1164.

Bowman, R. L., and Bowman, V. E. "Academic Courses to Train Resident Assistants." *NASPA Journal,* 1995, 36, 39–46.

Brillant, J. J., and Gribben, C. A. "A Workshop for Faculty and Counselors on Academic Dishonesty." *Journal of College Student Development,* 1993, 34, 437–438.

Brooks-Harris, J. E., and Stock-Ward, S. R. *Workshops: Designing and Facilitating Experiential Learning.* Thousand Oaks, Calif.: Sage, 1999.

Brown, S. "Student Affairs and Podcasting: The New Frontier?" *Student Affairs Online,* 7(2). [http://studentaffairs.com/ejournal/Summer_2006/StudentAffairsandPodcasting.htm]. 2006.

Burleson, B. R. "The Magic Bullet Model of Emotional Support: Analysis and Critique." Paper presented at the annual conference of the International Network of Personal Relationships, Norman, Okla., May 23–26, 1998.

Burleson, B. R. "Emotional Support Skill." In J. O. Greene and B. R. Burleson (eds.), *Handbook of Communication and Social Interaction Skills.* Mahwah, N.J.: Erlbaum, 2003.

Cardozo, P. J. "Dealing with the Angry Student: A Workshop for University Personnel." *Journal of College Student Personnel,* 1983, *24,* 166–167.

Denes-Raj, V., and Ehrlichman, H. "Effects of Premature Parental Death on Subjective Life Expectancy, Death Anxiety, and Health Behavior." *Omega,* 1991, *23,* 309–321.

DeSpelder, L. A., and Strickland, A. L. *The Last Dance: Encountering Death and Dying.* Mountain View, Calif.: Mayfield, 1996.

Doka, K. J. *Disenfranchised Grief: New Directions, Challenges, and Strategies for Practice.* Champaign, Ill.: Research Press, 2002.

Edmonds, S., and Hooker, K. "Perceived Changes in Life Meaning Following Bereavement." *Omega,* 1992, *25,* 307–318.

Evenbeck, S. E., and Jackson, B. "Faculty Development and the First Year." In M. L. Upcraft, J. N. Gardner, and B. O. Barefoot (eds.), *Challenging and Supporting the First-Year Student.* San Francisco: Jossey-Bass, 2005.

Gilbert, K. "Interactive Grief and Coping in the Marital Dyad." *Death Studies,* 1989, *13,* 605–626.

Godbey, R. *Enhancing Your Library's Public Relations with "Lunch-and-Learn" Workshops.* City and State and Office. 1996. (ED 399 963)

Hardison, H. G., Neimeyer, R. A., and Lichstein, K. L. "Insomnia and Complicated Grief Symptoms in Bereaved College Students." *Behavioral Sleep Medicine,* 2005, *3,* 99–111.

Jacoby, B. *The Student-as-Commuter: Developing a Comprehensive Institutional Response.* ASHE-ERIC Higher Education Report No. 7. Washington, D.C.: School of Education and Human Development, George Washington University, 1989.

James, J. W., and Friedman, R. *The Grief Recovery Handbook: The Action Program for Moving Beyond Death, Divorce, and Other Losses.* New York: HarperCollins, 1998.

Kadison, R., and DiGeronimo, T. F. *College of the Overwhelmed.* San Francisco: Jossey-Bass, 2004.

Meshot, C. M, and Leitner, L. M. "Death Threat, Parental Loss, and Interpersonal Style: A Personal Construct Investigation." *Death Studies,* 1994, *17,* 319–332.

Mosley, P. A. "Creating a Library Assignment Workshop for University Faculty." *Journal of Academic Librarianship,* 1998, *24,* 33–41.

Murray, J. L., Kagan, R. S., and Snider, B. R. "The Impact of Practical and Theoretical Training on Experienced and Inexperienced Peer Helpers." *Journal of Faculty Development,* 2001, *18,* 101–111.

Nathan. R. *My Freshman Year: What a Professor Learned by Becoming a Student.* Ithaca, N.Y.: Cornell University Press, 2005.

Neimeyer, R. A. (ed.). *Meaning Reconstruction and the Experience of Loss.* Washington, D.C.: American Psychological Association, 2001.

Oltjenbruns, K. A. "Positive Outcomes of Adolescents' Experience with Grief." *Journal of Adolescent Research,* 1991, *6,* 43–53.

Rack, J. J., Burleson, B. R., Bodie, G. D., Holmstrom, A. J., and Servaty-Seib, H. L. "Bereaved Adults' Evaluations of Grief Management Messages: Effects of Message Person Centeredness, Recipient Individual Differences, and Contextual Factors." *Death Studies,* forthcoming.

Rando, T. "Grief and Mourning: Accommodating to Loss." In H. Wass and R. A. Neimeyer (eds.), *Dying: Facing the Facts.* Philadelphia: Taylor & Francis, 1995.

Rickgarn, R.L.V. "The Need for Postvention on College Campuses: A Rationale and Case Study Findings." In C. A. Corr and D. E. Balk (eds.), *Handbook of Adolescent Death and Bereavement.* New York: Springer, 1996.

Rodolfa, E. R. "Training University Faculty to Assist Emotionally Troubled Students." *Journal of College Student Personnel,* 1987, *28,* 183–184.

Servaty-Seib, H. L., and Hamilton, L. A. "Educational Performance and Persistence of Bereaved College Students." *Journal of College Student Development,* 2006, *47,* 225–234.

Silverman, P. R. "The Impact of Parental Death on College-Age Women." *Psychiatric Clinics of North America*, 1987, *10*, 387–404.

Sklar, F., and Hartley, S. F. "Close Friends as Survivors: Bereavement Patterns in a 'Hidden' Population." *Omega*, 1990, *21*, 103–112.

Steufert, B. J. "Death on Campuses: Common Postvention Strategies in Higher Education." *Death Studies*, 2004, *28*, 151–172.

Twale, D. J., and Muse, V. "Resident Assistant Training Programs at Liberal Arts Colleges: Pre-Service and In-Service Options and RA Perceptions of Training." *College Student Journal*, 1996, *30*, 404–410.

Weslowski, M., Bowman, R. L., and Adams, V. "RA Training: A Comparison of Cognitive, Vicarious, and Experiential Modalities." *Journal of College and University Student Housing*, 1996, *26*, 30–38.

HEATHER L. SERVATY-SEIB *is associate professor of educational studies at Purdue University, first vice-president of the Association for Death Education, and a counseling psychologist in private practice.*

DEBORAH J. TAUB *is associate professor of higher education and coordinator of the graduate program in higher education at the University of North Carolina at Greensboro.*

6

Death by suicide can magnify and complicate bereavement, leaving community members struggling to sort through grief, anger, guilt, and the overwhelming feeling that they should somehow have been able to prevent the death.

Suicide and Its Impact on Campus

Heidi Levine

Although any death on campus can have profound effects on the community, leaving survivors to grope for meaning and cope with feelings of grief and loss, deaths by suicide entail several additional challenges. Shneidman (2001) estimated that an individual's suicide touches the lives of at least six others, creating wide-ranging psychological ripple effects among survivors. Shneidman suggested that in the wake of suicide, survivors are left to wonder what role they might have played in the death or whether there was something they could have done to prevent the suicide. In a college setting, it is likely that the number of people affected will be even greater than Shneidman's estimate, given the widespread patterns of interaction and connection found on campuses (Philip, 1990; Pruett, 1990; Rickgarn, 1994; Streufert, 2004; Webb, 1986).

The rate of death by suicide among college-age young adults has, after a slow rise, remained stable for more than twenty years (Schwartz, 2006). In the wake of several recent highly publicized cases, increasing attention has been paid to suicide prevention. Models, such as that developed and implemented at the University of Illinois (Pavela, 2006), focus on community education and identification of students at risk. The focus of this chapter is how campuses can respond effectively when suicides occur.

Reactions to Suicide

Although some aspects of survivors' grief following suicide are similar to other grief experiences (Clark, 2001), the intensity of these reactions can

be heightened due to the often unexpected nature of the death and the fact that the deceased is directly responsible for behavior leading to her or his own death, essentially committing a "self-murder" (Rickgarn, 1994). Similar to situations involving deaths in accidents, homicides, and other sudden deaths, the dominant initial responses to suicide are shock and confusion (Rickgarn, 1994). These feelings are complicated by survivors' perceptions that the individual wanted to die and acted toward that end, often lacking awareness of the ambivalence many suicidal people experience regarding the wish to die.

Another common—and often troubling—emotional response to suicide is anger toward the individual who has died (Parrish and Tunkle, 2005; Rickgarn, 1994). Although anger toward the deceased is not an unusual emotion associated with bereavement, the intensity of the anger in the case of suicide can be greater, due again to the fact that the individual has "chosen" to die. One factor complicating survivors' ability to deal with their anger can be the ambivalence that accompanies recognition of the fact that the suicide was likely the result of serious mental illness (Parrish and Tunkle, 2005). The guilt that survivors experience (Mauk and Rodgers, 1994; Rickgarn, 1994; Streufert, 2004) can also make the acknowledgment and expression of anger difficult. In the case of college student suicides, this anger is often projected onto the deceased's family, other friends, and the institution as a whole for not preventing the death (McIntosh and Kelly, 1992; Rickgarn, 1994).

Among the most markedly different responses between survivors of suicide and other deaths is a compelling need to find meaning in and reasons for the individual's death (McIntosh and Kelly, 1992; Parrish and Tunkle, 2005; Pruett, 1990). A long-lasting impact of suicide is the survivors' inability to know fully what led to the suicide (Pruett, 1990). Perhaps most personally damaging is the lingering question of whether there was anything the survivors could have done to prevent the death (McIntosh and Kelly, 1992; Pruett, 1990).

Suicide of Leaders

If any death by suicide leaves survivors struggling to make meaning of the death, suicide by individuals who are community leaders or role models intensifies the aftereffects. Survivors are left to wonder how they are supposed to deal with critical struggles and pain if models such as teachers, mentors, clergy, and professional helpers turn to suicide. Davis, Bates and Velasquez (1990) published a case study of the impacts of a faculty member's suicide on students and colleagues in a counselor education department. Although some responses depended on the survivor's relationship with the deceased (for example, attributing blame for departmental problems or harshly judging the deceased if the relationship had been strained), common reactions included anger—both at the deceased and at other faculty members—and guilt over having missed signs that the person was suicidal. For students in particular, a lingering sense of fear was a significant consequence of this event. Students were left questioning what this faculty member's action meant about the students' chosen profession, their academic program, and their own vulnerability to suicide.

Similar residual problems were described in a case study of patient reactions to the suicide of a therapist (Reynolds, Jennings, and Branson, 1997). Patients questioned the therapist's credibility, as reflected in one patient's comment that he "wasn't a very good therapist or this wouldn't have happened" (p. 178), and experienced feelings of personal abandonment. Even more distressing, patients struggled with feelings of depression, numbness, and hopelessness, and the authors found evidence that—due to the therapists' unique role and relationship with patients—the act may even have communicated that suicide is a reasonable solution to problems.

Individuals at Heightened Risk

Survivors are likely to experience significant and lasting negative effects related to others' suicides. Having a family member who died by suicide (Parrish and Tunkle, 2005) or simply knowing someone who has made an attempt may increase suicide risk (Hazell and Lewin, 1993); suicidal behavior on the part of close acquaintances and individuals seen as role models may lessen the perception of suicide as forbidden or taboo. Particular attention must be paid to the person or persons who found the body, who are likely to experience even greater levels of trauma than other survivors (Parrish and Tunkle, 2005).

Although the relationship with the deceased and the person's role in survivors' lives influence these aftereffects, other conditions may contribute to serious difficulties for survivors. Factors related to elevated suicide risk of survivors are histories of depression and substance abuse, impulsivity, history of family violence and sexual abuse, and prior suicidal behaviors (Hazell and Lewin, 1993; Mauk and Rodgers, 1994; Parrish and Tunkle, 2005). Therefore, students who are known to have experienced these risk factors should be assessed for increased risk in the aftermath of a suicide.

Mauk and Rodgers (1994), in their review of school-based postsuicide interventions, identified a number of additional risk factors related to survivors' experiences with the suicidal act. These factors include involvement in the suicide (for example, provided access to means), having prior knowledge about but not disclosing the plan to adults or other authorities, and having served in a "therapist" role with the deceased. Other factors focused on the relationship between the deceased and survivor, including the survivor's identification with the deceased's situation or feelings of guilt about some aspect of their relationship.

In addition, Mauk and Rodgers (1994) identified the following barriers to adolescents seeking help in the aftermath of suicide: lack of knowledge about available resources, difficulty expressing thoughts and feelings about the suicide, fear that seeking help indicates weakness, and a desire to protect themselves and their family from pain associated with their inner experiences. Awareness of such barriers can be useful when developing plans to respond to suicide.

Philip (1990) described the feelings of helplessness and passivity that are common among suicide survivors on college campuses. He suggested that survivors need help decreasing their sense of victimization and increasing recognition of their potential agency instrumentality and vitality. In light of survivors' frequent fear and need to externalize blame for the death (Davis, Bates, and Velasquez, 1990), it also is important that campus officials demonstrate that there are competent adults in charge who are taking care of things on campus.

Protective Factors

Although campus officials must recognize individual characteristics and factors that lead to heightened risk in the aftermath of suicides, awareness of factors that might protect students from increased risk is also essential. One of the qualities found to buffer adverse reactions to traumatic incidents is holding well-developed spiritual beliefs and practices (Lee and Waters, 2003). Certain personality traits (including optimism and extroversion) and the interaction between personality and environment have also been connected to the degree of resilience individuals exhibit in stressful circumstances. Teaching and encouraging students to focus on controllable aspects of life, engage directly in problem solving, find healthy ways to calm anxieties, and challenge distortedly negative thought patterns can help foster resilience in highly stressful situations.

Among the most important characteristics of resilient individuals are the ability and willingness to reach out to others for support (Riolli, Savicki, and Cepani, 2002). McNally, Bryant, and Ehlers (2003), in their review of responses to traumatic events, identified as chief among natural coping behaviors the tendency to seek support from family and friends. They found that most people derived more benefit from connecting with these sources of support than from more formal or structured interventions. In fact, the authors stressed the importance of recognizing the normality of most expressions of grief and distress in the face of trauma. Campus officials should communicate information about loss to students (and others) and not rush to disrupt normal grief reactions. Structured interventions should be used with individuals who are at elevated risk of developing significant problems or for whom natural coping responses are inadequate (McNally, Bryant, and Ehlers, 2003).

Postvention

Postvention refers to a series of intentional and therapeutic interventions made to survivors in the wake of critical incidents such as suicide. Among the first tasks necessary for implementing these efforts is to identify the individuals and groups most affected by the suicide (Hazell and Lewin, 1993; Jobes, Luoma, Hustead, and Mann, 2000; Pruett, 1990; Rickgarn, 1994). Although Shneidman (2001) estimated that each suicide affects at least six other individuals directly, some researchers suggest that the web of suicide survivors is much broader, extending to classmates, organization members, and distant acquaintances (Pruett, 1990; Rickgarn, 1994). The task of identifying students in need of assistance is often made more difficult because those "in need" are self-defined and may not be obvious to others (Jobes, Luoma, Hustead, and Mann, 2000).

Postsuicide interventions are one of three integral components of a school-based suicide prevention program: "inoculation" (prevention), crisis intervention (identifying and assisting individuals at elevated risk), and postvention (Celotta, 1995). The focus of assistance following a suicide should be helping individual members and the community as a whole adjust; such efforts must occur concurrently with any crisis intervention efforts. The most immediate goals of postsuicide intervention efforts are to facilitate the healing process for the institution and its members and decrease the risk of suicide contagion. A third, longer-term goal is to encourage new growth, such as the development of new policies and procedures. A four-year study tracking high schools that had experienced suicides found no additional suicides in schools where psychologist-led interventions took place (Poijula, Wahlberg, and Dyregrov, 2001). However, in the school where appropriate intervention did not occur, another suicide occurred within two months.

Postvention Components. Postsuicide outreach efforts have been described as a form of "psychological first aid," providing immediate and brief assistance to students and others affected by the death (Streufert, 2004) and assisting participants to begin expressing their feelings, share memories of the deceased, and begin the long process of striving to understand what has happened. Among the factors that contribute to psychological difficulties following trauma is a lack of social support. In a setting such as a college campus—where members of an extended community are affected by traumatic events, initiatives that build on and enhance a sense of group cohesion can be important tools in fostering effective coping (McNally, Bryant, and Ehlers, 2003).

Parrish and Tunkle (2005) provide general recommendations regarding postsuicide intervention in public education settings, many of which are applicable to college and university campuses. First, campus officials must respond to the community quickly, preferably within twenty-four hours of the suicide. Although discussions should not focus on specific and detailed features of the suicide event (Celotta, 1995) (which might serve as suggestions to others at heightened risk), dispelling rumors and allaying fears require accurate information. Outreach should be made to faculty and staff, as well as to students, particularly those in the academic department of the deceased or those who had close relationships with the deceased, such as an organization adviser or residence life supervisor.

Discussions should emphasize that although thoughts about death are normal, suicide is not a normal or healthy response to situational stressors (Celotta, 1995). Although significant stresses (such as the loss of a relationship or academic or legal problems) might precede a suicide attempt, the presence of preexisting psychological problems—in addition to and beyond any situational factors—is responsible for the decreased adaptive coping abilities that lead to suicidal behaviors (Celotta, 1995). Addressing the connection of mental illness to suicide directly can also help mitigate stigma and feelings of shame survivors may have about their own needs and encourage them to seek help (Parrish and Tunkle, 2005). By framing suicidal thoughts and feelings as a common by-product of conditions such as depression, survivors have greater potential to move from viewing suicidal ideation as indicative of being like the deceased (perhaps selfish or doomed) to seeing treatment as offering hope for restoring well-being.

Because at-risk survivors are not always easily identified, some type of brief screening instruments might be used in targeted areas (such as residence halls, classes, or organizations to which the deceased belonged) to help identify at-risk individuals (Hazell and Lewin, 1993). Potential areas to be assessed could include whether students have any personal friends who have survived suicide attempts in the past twelve months or died as a result of suicide, as well as questions addressing their own mental health (for example, "I frequently feel sad, depressed, and unhappy") and whether they have thought about self-harm or tried to hurt or kill themselves.

Above all, the event must not be glamorized or romanticized in any way (Parrish and Tunkle, 2005). Care must be taken to avoid presenting the deceased as a tragic hero and to emphasize that the death was unnecessary. Disruptions in the regular routine of the campus contributes to a sense of prominence around the suicide. Therefore, the campus must balance taking an active role in providing opportunities for individuals and groups to process the event with the resumption of its normal schedule and functions as soon as possible (Celotta, 1995; Webb, 1986).

Caveats. Although widely accepted, the effectiveness of debriefing and related group interventions (such as critical incident stress management) has come into question; when not conducted properly, such approaches can make the situation worse. Although participants often report benefits to having the opportunity to express their emotions following difficult experiences, some researchers have suggested that the long-term effects of these interventions may be negligible (McNally, Bryant, and Ehlers, 2003; Zech and Rimé, 2005). One concern raised about debriefing strategies is that people's natural recovery processes, which include the gradual processing of intensely painful memories and affect, can be overwhelmed by being forced to delve into the expression of these feelings immediately (McNally, Bryant, and Ehlers, 2003). Activities such as peer-led group debriefings and discussions that take place without concomitant crisis intervention or focus on suicide prevention have the capacity to increase the risk of imitative acts by students who are themselves at risk (Celotta, 1995).

Callahan (1996) provided consultation to a school district that had experienced apparent suicide clusters following the unrelated suicides of two middle-school-age students. Although his consultation and review dealt with a much younger cohort than college students, his findings are instructive for higher education. After each of the two initial suicides (which occurred within two months of each other, by students who did not know each other), debriefing and other activities, including the establishment of support groups for students, took place. Students who became upset were allowed to leave classes to speak with a counselor. These activities continued for several weeks, fostering a "romanticized and melodramatic" (p. 111) atmosphere.

Over the following six months, a significant spike in suicide-related hospitalizations and suicide attempts in this age group occurred. The group of students who were close friends of the second suicide began acting out, engaging in suicidal and self-injurious behaviors (such as cutting themselves without suicidal intent), and there was evidence of a suicide pact between two girls. Driving these maladaptive behaviors were secondary gains of elevated status and attention among close friends of the deceased, as well as benefits from the loosening of normal boundaries, such as allowing students to speak with counselors at any time for extended periods, thereby missing classes frequently.

Among the findings of the consultation was that special activities went on too long following the deaths. Group, rather than individual, support processes also seemed to intensify participants' feelings, increased the glamorizing of suicide and promoted participants' identification with the deceased. The extended focus on the suicides appeared to activate emotional distress and difficulties coping among a group who had experienced psychological and emotional difficulties in the past.

Outcomes of the consultation included requiring students who wanted to speak with counselors to do so by appointment, as well as the development of policies and procedures that established consequences for students who engaged in suicidal talk and gestures. Overall, the activities undertaken by this district led to the inadvertent normalization of suicidal ideation and behavior, and they demonstrate how easily well-intentioned but not carefully developed efforts can contribute to suicide contagion. In the college setting, postsuicide intervention activities must be planned carefully and implemented by professionals with a full understanding of suicide assessment and prevention rather than by peers and paraprofessionals.

Preventing Contagion

The Callahan (1996) case study points to several features of well-developed programs that can decrease the likelihood of imitative suicidal behaviors: returning quickly to normal activities, minimizing opportunities for individuals to romanticize or glorify either the suicidal act or the deceased, and creating parameters around the response to suicidal behaviors. Emphasizing the role of underlying psychological disorders and framing suicide explicitly as an abnormal response to stress can also decrease contagion (Poijula, Wahlberg, and Dyregrov, 2001).

The Centers for Disease Control and Prevention (CDC, 1994) published recommendations on the role of media reporting in preventing suicide contagion. These recommendations were based on the CDC's 1992 review of youth suicide patterns and prevention programs spanning four decades and focused on firmly established findings that sensational and overly detailed reporting of suicides contributed significantly to imitative acts. Among the CDC's suggested reporting and media guidelines are these:

1. Information should be conveyed in an efficient and accurate manner,
2. Media representatives should be provided with information regarding suicide contagion and how to limit potential effects.
3. The cause of suicide should be presented as multifaceted and not as the result of a single event or problem.
4. Excessive details about the event or method or otherwise sensationalizing or romanticizing the suicide should be avoided.
5. Reports of public displays of grief should be minimized to avoid glorification.
6. Suicide should never be portrayed as a successful means of having dealt with or resolved a problem.

Refusing to speak with the media is generally unhelpful, as it creates an adversarial relationship, and opportunities for education and outreach are missed.

Campus Guidelines

The CDC (1994) guidelines for media response to suicide are adaptable to campus response plans. Campus officials in contact with external media should be aware of the CDC guidelines, ensure that their statements and actions are in accordance with the CDC recommendations, and share with members of the media information related to sensationalized reports and suicide contagion. On some campuses, a more significant challenge can arise when dealing with student newspapers and other campus media. Student reporters, unlike their professional counterparts, may have difficulty understanding limits on information that can be shared and are more apt to have access to and report on campus rumors, thereby setting or exacerbating a contagion-fostering tone.

Preventing suicide contagion or imitative acts must be the primary focus of a college counseling center response to suicide (Philip, 1990). Philip suggested that while recognizing the importance of allowing students to set the agenda to address their feelings and needs, institutions must minimize events such as memorials or funerals that elevate or glorify the suicide. Additional campus recommendations include not publishing details about the death (including any suicide note) or pictures of the deceased (Streufert, 2004). Although limiting unofficial and spontaneous student memorials always has posed challenges, managing this aspect of student response is even more complex in the current electronic milieu. Fully controlling or even being fully aware of student blogs and Web sites paying tribute to the deceased or discussing the suicidal act is beyond any institution's ability. This emphasizes the importance of engaging in timely and widespread educational efforts focusing on factors related to suicide, including directly addressing suicide contagion.

Model Responses

To help ensure that campus responses are effective, response plans and protocols must be developed in advance of an actual crisis (Philip, 1990; Streufert, 2004). Some colleges and universities have developed response protocols that can serve as models for other campuses wishing to develop or review their suicide response plans. Rickgarn (1994) identified a series of questions that can guide the development of response protocols, focusing primarily on the identification of which offices will be responsible for managing tasks following a suicide (or other student death). These areas include notifying family, contacting other offices and agencies involved with postsuicide intervention and other immediate activities, communicating with the campus and the media, securing the deceased's personal effects, coordinating with local police, reassigning roommates or suitemates if the death occurred in a residence hall, and coordinating campus debriefing activities (see Chapter Eight).

Defusing and *debriefing* are two different but important components of responding to suicide (Pruett, 1990). Defusing should take place as soon after the event as possible, providing closely affected community members an opportunity to express and receive support in dealing with their immediate reactions. In residence halls, the staff must be debriefed first and provided with support and resources as they prepare to reach out to residents. If available, clergy members can be excellent resources in these situations.

Debriefing sessions should take place within a few days of the suicide and involve a wider range of participants. As with defusing, part of the goal of debriefing sessions is allowing participants to address their feelings about the suicide; debriefings follow an educational model, stressing the underlying mental health issues discussed earlier and providing information about resources. Keeping in mind that many individuals beyond the deceased's immediate circle will be affected by the suicide, multiple debriefing sessions should be held, reaching out to such groups as academic departments, athletic teams, and campus organizations.

NEW DIRECTIONS FOR STUDENT SERVICES • DOI: 10.1002/ss

Response Teams

One way to help ensure the development and implementation of comprehensive response plan is through the use of death response teams (DRTs), a model that has been effective both beyond (Campbell, Cataldie, McIntosh, and Millet, 2004) and within higher education settings (Rickgarn, 1994; Streufert, 2004). Teams of eight to ten members should include representation from across the campus and should mirror the ethnic diversity of the campus to maximize familiarity with different cultural groups' understandings about and responses to death. Team members might take specific roles or areas of responsibility, such as coordinator and liaisons to family, media, and the community. Given the likelihood of increased demand on campus counseling services created by a campus death, Streufert (2004) recommends that the DRT coordinator not be a member of the counseling staff.

These response teams should be prepared and empowered to address the following aspects of a campus suicide response: outreach to affected student, faculty, and staff groups; contact with area media; planning any campus-based memorial activities; and working with the family (Streufert, 2004). In each of these areas, guidelines to prevent contagion should be followed. If bereavement support groups are offered, potential members should be screened to rule out participation by students who are inappropriate (for example, experiencing active suicidal ideation or with a history of multiple losses). Students who are excluded from support groups should be offered the opportunity to engage in individual counseling. Another DRT facet merits additional focus: memorial services.

Memorials after suicide present a special challenge to colleges and universities. Students are likely to express a strong desire to find a way to memorialize their deceased friend, teammate, or classmate. Memorials, however, have a high potential for presenting the death and the individual in an idealized light—a condition that can contribute to suicide contagion (CDC, 1994). To minimize contagion, campus memorials might take the form of contributions to mental health and suicide prevention organizations or campus scholarships. Memorial services, if held, should stress the unnecessary nature of the death and provide information related to prevention.

Psychological Autopsy

Shortly after the initial postvention, conducting a psychological autopsy can be an extremely useful tool for helping campuses assess their response and identify any troubling behavior patterns that might be emerging among students (Grieger and Greene, 1998). The psychological autopsy involves a thorough review of records and facts related to the suicide, leading to the construction of a profile of the individual and event. The autopsy requires participants to look at the campus as a whole, giving administrators a systemic perspective of the incident. In their description of how a psychological autopsy was conducted on one campus, Grieger and Greene reported on the identification of factors that seemed to contribute to a climate that encouraged suicide and identified possible contagion within close clusters of students.

Objectives of the autopsy are to develop a narrative of events, review actions taken, gather data regarding the incident (including demographic information, antecedents, and campus factors), and develop recommendations regarding prevention and future postvention. In addition, the autopsy can serve as an opportunity for debriefing the professional staff who were closely involved with the incident. To engage in a meaningful review, the team conducting the autopsy must be sensitive to how information about the person and event will be shared, and confidentiality within the team must be maintained.

Final Thoughts

Although any death on campus creates profound ripple effects, deaths by suicide bring unique challenges to a community. Common survivor reactions, such as anger and guilt, are often intensified (McIntosh and Kelly, 1992; Parrish and Tunkle, 2005; Pruett, 1990; Rickgarn, 1994). The needs to identify someone to blame (Parrish and Tunkle, 2005; Rickgarn, 1994) and understand what could have driven someone to an act of self-murder (McIntosh and Kelly, 1992; Parrish and Tunkle, 2005; Pruett, 1990) are perhaps the most distinct reactions to suicide. These reactions may be complicated by leadership roles on the part of the deceased (Davis, Bates, and Velasquez, 1990; Reynolds, Jennings, and Branson, 1997) and by survivors' own experiences with depression and suicidal feelings (Hazell and Lewin, 1993; Mauk and Rodgers, 1994; Parrish and Tunkle, 2005).

Responding to suicide requires quick identification of those most closely affected and significantly at risk (Hazell and Lewin, 1993; Jobes, Luoma, Hustead, and Mann, 2000; Pruett, 1990; Rickgarn, 1994), reaching out to provide accurate information and opportunities for survivors to process their thoughts and feelings. Facilitating connections among survivors can help foster natural healing mechanisms (McNally, Bryant, and Ehlers, 2003) and bolster the coping abilities of those who are most intensely affected and at heightened risk. Support balanced with avoidance of sensationalizing or romanticizing the death and making clear the role of mental illness in suicidal acts are hallmarks of campuses that are sensitive to community needs and unlikely to contribute to suicide contagion (Callahan, 1996; Jobes, Luoma, Hustead, and Mann, 2000; Phillip, 1990; Streufert, 2004). In the midst of this outreach, members of the campus community must attend to the needs of the caretakers, who are often emotionally depleted in the aftermath of suicide (Parrish and Tunkle, 2005; Pruett, 1990). Particularly in need of opportunities to obtain their own support and debriefing are mental health professionals who have provided treatment to the deceased (Parrish and Tunkle, 2005).

NEW DIRECTIONS FOR STUDENT SERVICES • DOI: 10.1002/ss

Exhibit 6.1. Suicide Postvention Checklist

__ Notify campus officials
__ Activate death response team or other essential personnel
__ Contact family
    __ Offer condolences
    __ Provide information factually
    __ Offer assistance with arrangements
    __ Follow up
__ Contact police; assist police with filing and processing reports
__ Identify and notify closely affected individuals and groups
    __ Residence hall staff
    __ Roommates and suitemates
    __ Academic adviser
    __ Teammates and organization members
__ Identify and follow up with other individuals known to be at risk
__ Hold one or more defusing sessions within twenty-four hours
__ Hold one or more debriefing sessions within seventy-two hours
__ Contact the media
    __ Provide appropriate, factual information
    __ Share guidelines on minimizing contagion
__ Provide crisis intervention counseling and assessment
__ Assist students with planning appropriate memorial activities
__ Debrief the response team and other caretakers

Exhibit 6.1 presents a sample checklist that campus officials might use to help identify and track response activities following suicide. This particular list assumes that a campus has established a death response team; campuses without DRTs would need to build in steps to identify the campus officials who should be involved in responding to suicide. In addition, checklists should be individualized to take into account aspects of the campus culture, established relationships with campus ministry or area clergy, and campus traditions that should be respected. Officials may also need to modify a plan to incorporate working around a designated crime scene.

Perhaps more important than following specific, individual steps is for campus constituencies to come together in planning and managing their response. Campuses that are most successful in dealing with suicides in a compassionate, thorough, and nonescalating manner are those that work from a team approach, coordinating activities and response teams representing the breadth of the community (Mitchell, Elmore, and Fygetakis, 1996; Philip, 1990; Pruett, 1990; Rickgarn, 1994; Streufert, 2004).

References

Callahan, J. "Negative Effects of a School Suicide Postvention Program: A Case Example." *Crisis*, 1996, *17*, 108–115.

Campbell, F. R., Cataldie, L., McIntosh, J., and Millet, K. "An Active Postvention Program." *Crisis*, 2004, *25*, 30–32.

Celotta, B. "The Aftermath of Suicide: Postvention in a School Setting." *Journal of Mental Health Counseling*, 1995, *17*, 397–412.

Centers for Disease Control and Prevention. *Youth Suicide Prevention Programs: A Resource Guide.* Atlanta: U.S. Department of Health and Human Services, 1992.

Centers for Disease Control and Prevention. *Morbidity and Mortality Weekly Report*, Vol. 43. Atlanta: U.S. Department of Health and Human Services, 1994.

Clark, S. "Bereavement After Suicide: How Far Have We Come and Where Do We Go from Here?" *Crisis*, 2001, *23*, 102–108.

Davis, J. M., Bates, C., and Velasquez, R. J. "Faculty Suicide: Guidelines for Effective Coping with a Suicide in a Counselor-Training Program." *Counselor Education and Supervision*, 1990, *29*, 197–204.

Grieger, I., and Greene, P. "The Psychological Autopsy as a Tool in Student Affairs." *Journal of College Student Development*, 1998, *39*, 388–392.

Hazell, P., and Lewin, T. "An Evaluation of Postvention Following Adolescent Suicide." *Suicide and Life-Threatening Behavior*, 1993, *23*, 101–109.

Jobes, D. A., Luoma, J. B., Hustead, L.A.T., and Mann, R. E. "In the Wake of Suicide: Survivorship and Postvention." In R. W. Maris, A. L. Berman, and M. M. Silverman (eds.), *Comprehensive Textbook of Suicidology.* New York: Guilford Press, 2000.

Lee, S. S., and Waters, C. "Impact of Stressful Life Experiences and of Spiritual Well-Being on Trauma Symptoms." *Journal of Prevention and Intervention in the Community*, 2003, *26*, 39–47.

Mauk, G. W., and Rodgers, P. L. "Building Bridges over Troubled Waters: School-Based Postvention with Adolescent Survivors of Peer Suicide." *Crisis Intervention*, 1994, *1*, 103–123.

McIntosh, J. L., and Kelly, L. D. "Survivors' Reactions: Suicide vs. Other Causes." *Journal of Crisis Intervention and Suicide Prevention*, 1992, *13*, 82–93.

McNally, R. J., Bryant, R. A., and Ehlers, A. "Does Early Psychological Intervention Promote Recovery from Posttraumatic Stress?" *Psychological Science in the Public Interest*, 2003, *4*, 45–79.

Mitchell, S. L., Elmore, K., and Fygetakis, L. M. "A Coordinated Campus Response to Student Suicide." *Journal of College Student Development*, 1996, *37*, 698–699.

Parrish, M., and Tunkle, J. "Clinical Challenges Following an Adolescent's Death by Suicide: Bereavement Issued Faced by Family, Friends, Schools, and Clinicians." *Clinical Social Work Journal*, 2005, *33*, 81–102.

Pavela, G. "Should Colleges Withdraw Students Who Threaten or Attempt Suicide?" *Journal of American College Health*, 2006, *54*, 367–371.

Philip, A. F. "Suicide and Suicidal Behavior: Postvention—Counseling Center Response." In *College Student Suicide*, New York: Haworth Press, 1990.

Poijula, S., Wahlberg, K., and Dyregrov, A. "Adolescent Suicide and Suicide Contagion in Three Secondary Schools." *International Journal of Emergency Mental Health*, 2001, *3*, 163–168.

Pruett, H. L. *Crisis Intervention and Prevention with Suicide.* New Directions for Student Services, no. 49. San Francisco: Jossey-Bass, 1990.

Reynolds, J., Jennings, G., and Branson, M. L. "Patients' Reactions to the Suicide of a Psychotherapist." *Suicide and Life-Threatening Behavior*, 1997, *27*, 176–181.

Rickgarn, R.L.V. *Perspectives on College Suicide.* Amityville, N.Y.: Baywood, 1994.

Riolli, L., Savicki, V., and Cepani, A. "Resilience in the Face of Catastrophe: Optimism, Personality, and Coping in the Kosovo Crisis." *Journal of Applied Social Psychology*, 2002, *32*, 1604–1627.

Schwartz, A. J. "College Student Suicide in the United States, 1990–1991 Through 2003–2004." *Journal of American College Health*, 2006, *54*, 341–352.

Shneidman, E. S. *Comprehending Suicide: Landmarks in 20th-Century Suicidology.* Washington, D.C.: American Psychological Association, 2001.

Streufert, B. J. "Death on Campuses: Common Postvention Strategies in Higher Education." *Death Studies,* 2004, *28,* 151–172.

Webb, N. B. "Before and After Suicide: A Preventive Outreach Program for Colleges." *Suicide and Life-Threatening Behavior,* 1986, *16,* 469–480.

Zech, E., and Rimé, B. "Is Talking About an Emotional Experience Helpful? Effects on Emotional Recovery and Perceived Benefits." *Clinical Psychology and Psychotherapy,* 2005, *12,* 270–287.

HEIDI LEVINE is director of the Health and Counseling Department at the State University of New York at Geneseo.

7

This chapter offers student affairs professionals suggestions for notifying students of deaths in their families and notifying campus community and family members of student deaths.

Guidelines for Death Notification in College Student Populations

Lou Ann Hamilton

College is a time for intellectual growth and also an important time for psychological and emotional maturation and the development of coping skills. The death loss of a family member or friend is a relatively common experience for college students (see Chapter One). How students and family members are notified of a death can have a long-standing impact on their grief and subsequent functioning, as well as potential ramifications for the institution.

Three topics related to the process of death notification are addressed in this chapter: notifying a student of the death of a family member or friend, notifying family members (including spouses, parents, and perhaps siblings) of a student's death, and self-care (efforts aimed at maintaining mental and physical health) recommendations for campus professionals who have responsibility for death notification. The way a student is informed of a death loss has implications for the student's adjustment and retention and how the individual copes with the loss in the future (Lord, 2000; Stewart, 1999). Communicating with family members after the death of a student is a sensitive task that not only involves the family's immediate reactions but also has the potential to affect the entire university (in situations where litigation could arise). Because death notification is an emotionally demanding activity, the responsible professional is at risk for burnout (a condition characterized by mental and physical exhaustion). To avoid burnout, the individual who delivers this type of news must learn to practice good self-care. Throughout this chapter, compassion and the practical

NEW DIRECTIONS FOR STUDENT SERVICES, no. 121, Spring 2008 © Wiley Periodicals, Inc.
Published online in Wiley InterScience (www.interscience.wiley.com) • DOI: 10.1002/ss.268

aspects of death notification are emphasized. Note that the information and recommendations offered here are based primarily on my own experiences in my work at Purdue, supported by professional resources focused on the process of death notification.

Notifying Students of the Death of a Loved One

The process whereby college students are informed of the death of a loved one depends on many factors. In today's technological society, students are easily accessible. Because of the widespread use of cell phones and other portable electronic devices, family members of many students are able to contact students immediately. Consequently, during the evening hours, students are typically notified of family death losses by family members. During class hours, however, when students may have their phones turned off, family members often seek other ways of contacting students in emergency situations. The office of the dean of students or other student affairs offices (for example, residential life or advising offices) might be notified that a student's family is trying to reach the student with bad news. Many practical and specific issues should be kept in mind when interacting with family members who are attempting to contact a student in death-related situations.

First, verify that the person calling to report the death is indeed who he or she claims to be (Brooks and others, 1992). Difficulties can arise if such precautions are not taken. It is best to verify information independently. For example, when a call comes into the Office of the Dean of Students at Purdue University, the protocol is to get as much information as possible from the caller, including the telephone number of the hospital or family member. Following the call, the student affairs professional then calls the police or the coroner to establish as many facts as possible, such as the cause of death.

Make certain, too, that the correct student is being notified; otherwise, errors can lead to unnecessary distress or even trauma (Brooks and others, 1992). Verification can be established by asking the caller to provide personal information that can be confirmed in the student's record (middle name, home address, identification number, and so on). Particularly on a large campus, there may be students with the same name or similar names. As important as it is to give death notification in a timely manner, it is even more important to verify the facts of the case before proceeding.

After the identity of the person sought has been verified, a plan for how to proceed with the death notification must be determined (see Iserson, 1999; Leash, 1994; Stevenson, 1995). The following aspects of that plan are of greatest importance.

Who Should Do the Notification. Whenever possible, go in a team of two (Brooks and others, 1992). There is no way to know how an individual will respond to the news that someone has died, regardless of whether the death was somewhat expected or unexpected. One member of the team should be prepared to handle the emotional issues and be available to stay with the student as a support until someone close to the student arrives. The other member of the team should be available to make phone calls or take care of other more matter-of-fact duties such as contacting roommates or friends and engaging them in support of the bereaved student (Brooks and others, 1992), notifying instructors that the student will not be in class for several days, or arranging for transportation to the student's residence if the meeting takes place elsewhere. If the student should faint or collapse, one team member can stay with the student while the other team member calls for medical support.

Campus professionals engaged in death notification must not make assumptions regarding the reactions of the recipients to the bad news. If students remain calm and unemotional, do not assume that they are coping well. It is still important to attempt to find a friend, roommate, or other support person to be with the person when the campus professionals leave. Goodrum (2005), referring to the reactions of those notified of death losses, points out that the "numbness (or shock) . . . represents an overpowering feeling state, not an absence of feeling" (p. 146).

Where the Student Should Be Notified. The first step in contacting the student is to examine the student's schedule and then determine where and when to meet. If the student does not have a class scheduled, the campus professionals might need to go to the student's residence. If the schedule indicates that the student should be in class, go to the classroom building, locate the classroom, and then arrange for a quiet office nearby. If no office is available, an empty classroom will do, as long as one of the team members has a telephone. The student should be able to call home or call the hospital to speak with a family member immediately. Other items to bring include tissues and business cards. Students notified of death losses can be expected to be overwhelmed by emotion and are not likely to remember the names of the individuals who assisted with notification.

Team members should not meet the student and then walk together to their own offices to deliver the notification. Although intended as a supportive effort, the long walk and the delay will likely create more anxiety for the student (Brooks and others, 1992). If the student is not in class, the campus professionals should go to the student's official address and make every attempt to speak with the student at home. If the student cannot be located, inform family members promptly that the death notification did not take place.

Making the Notification. It is preferable to go to the student's classroom before class begins rather than at the end of the class. A team member can ask the instructor to have the student meet with representatives from the office of the dean of students in the hallway before class begins. The team should make sure that the student brings all books and other belongings when leaving the classroom. Although prior to class is optimal, sometimes it is necessary to meet the student after class. The team should not interrupt the class but should step in just before adjournment of the class and ask to speak with the student. When the student joins the team, introductions can be made, and the student can be asked to accompany the team to the prearranged nearby location.

In private, team members should reintroduce themselves and verify that the student is in fact the person to be notified. In a small college, a member of the death notification team might recognize the student, whereas in a very large university, it is unlikely that the team will know the student. The staff member who will be the main emotional support should reveal the death loss information calmly but clearly (Leash, 1994). Professionals should avoid beginning with statements such as "I have bad news" or "I'm sorry but . . ." (p. 52). Instead, start notifications with a statement such as "We need to talk to you about your grandfather." Do not prolong the process (Brooks and others, 1992), but make gentle statements such as "Your grandfather died this morning of a heart attack." Use the words *died, dead,* and *death* rather than euphemisms such *passed away* or *passed on* to be sure everyone understands the reality of the event (Stewart, 1999; Stone, 2007). It may be necessary to repeat information to the student until the reality sinks in.

Avoid making assumptions about the relationship the student had with the deceased. Although the death of a grandparent or an aunt or uncle may be assumed to have less impact than that of a parent or a spouse, the student may have been raised by or in the same home as the deceased and feel especially close. In addition, past losses can affect a student's reaction to a current death loss. For example, during one death notification, a student burst into tears when I told him that his brother had died. He explained that his brother had been his only surviving immediate family member, as his parents were also deceased. This situation intensified when a phone call made to his aunt revealed that the death was a suicide. In contrast to this situation, there are times when students are calm and seem somewhat prepared for the death. However, make certain that the student has a support system, and ensure that that support network has been activated.

Follow-Up. When the notification has been completed, the campus professional should return to the office and implement follow-up activities as permitted by campus regulations (Stone, 2007). Examples of such follow-up activities include letters of absence sent to the student's instructors and adviser and a letter sent to the student with an offer to help, along with other referral sources on campus for when the student returns. The importance of acknowledgment and recognition by a compassionate and caring staff member cannot be overemphasized. Such support can decrease the experience of disenfranchised grief (Doka, 2002) and help the student assimilate back into academic activities.

Few campuses actually have bereavement policies for students, although such policies are standard in most employment settings, including those of university and college faculty and staff (Servaty-Seib and Hamilton, 2006). An exception is the policy that has been developed and implemented at Ball State University. According to this policy, students have rights that dictate how many days they may be excused for a death, depending on how far they must travel and their relationship to the deceased. Upon their return to campus, students provide documentation to each instructor, who will retroactively excuse the students from class and allow them to make up the work missed.

The lack of policies to protect the rights of bereaved students highlights the need for campus professionals to be proactive and speak on behalf of students. Although it seems logical that faculty members and campus regulations would support students at a time of loss, such support is not forthcoming in all situations.

Notification of a Student Death

When a student dies, notifying family members can be a daunting task. It is a sensitive issue that can affect long-term perceptions of the institution while also setting the tone for the grief process. Although it may be difficult at the time of a student's death to remain mindful of how family members will regard the institution, this issue must be considered.

Campus professionals may be more or less involved in the notification process when a student death has occurred. Who informs the family of the death loss is frequently dictated by how the death occurs. Often the college or university will not be the actual notifier in the case of a student's death. Usually the hospital or law enforcement agency handling the death will be in charge of the actual death notification. The institution of higher education may be approached by one of these agencies as they work to acquire family contact information. The hospital or police will verify the identity of the deceased, but the campus professional must make sure to give out the correct information by checking any identification numbers or identifying details the agency provides against campus information. As noted earlier, at a large university, there can be several students with the same name or similar names. Some things to check are driver's license or student identification number that was recovered with the student's body, the correct spelling of names, local and home addresses, and middle name or initial.

If the institution of higher education is in charge of notifying the parents, campus professionals must take the same precautions and steps to verify the identity of the student who has died. If at all possible, the team should travel to the family's home to provide the news of the death (Brooks and others, 1992), equipped with as many details of the death as are available. If the deceased was attending college far from his or her family, however, travel to the family home might not be feasible. Telephone notification should be considered if the family lives more than one hour from the institution (Leash, 1994). Telephone notification may be appropriate so that the family can be informed of the death in a timely manner and are also able to make any necessary travel plans as promptly as possible. If the family is not available, do not leave a voice-mail message. The most appropriate strategy is for the campus professional to continue calling until reaching the person or persons listed as the student's next of kin.

When delivering a death notification by phone, the caller must make sure that he or she is talking to the correct family member. Ask questions such as "Are you the parent of Sally, who is a student at this university and is majoring in . . . ?" Tell the next of kin that his or her relative has been in an accident or is at the hospital (giving the name and phone number of the hospital). The campus professional must then assess if the family member is alone or is with others who can be of support. If he or she is alone, ask the next of kin to contact another family member or friend to keep him or her company. Explain that the staff member will try to get more information about the student and will call back when that support person is present.

When it is clear that the next of kin is with others who can be of support, offer the death notification in a gentle and straightforward manner (Brooks and others, 1992). Possible language includes "Your husband has died in an automobile accident" or "Your daughter was found dead this morning in her room." Give simple details; do not ever mislead or lie (Brooks and others, 1992). It is sometimes tempting to refrain from providing all the facts to families in an attempt to avoid traumatizing them. However, that is neither the role nor the right of the campus professional, and such an approach is likely to create hard feelings and a sense of betrayal for the family in the long run. Most people simply want the truth and have a need to know as much as possible about the last hours of their loved one's life. If details are suppressed, family members may conclude that the institution has something to hide.

When death notification is handled in an honest, caring, and forthright way, families are often left with a feeling of great respect for the institution. This is a moment they will remember for the rest of their lives and is a critical juncture in their feelings toward the institution. Families will experience tremendous sadness but can also be left with a sense of having been treated with respect. The verbal and nonverbal actions of student affairs professionals have the power to communicate that the student's life had meaning and that the deceased was an important member of the institutional community. In contrast, if family members are told of the student's death in a cold and heartless manner, they may blame the institution and feel disrespect and resentment. Stewart (1999) emphasizes both the *process* (the manner) and the *content* (the information) of death notification. In addition, as representatives of the university, campus professionals can and should express sympathy but must not address the issue of responsibility for the incident.

Even if the institution of higher education is not handling the death notification, the family must be contacted by someone from the campus shortly after the death with condolences and an offer to facilitate communication between the institution and the family. Campus professionals can foster goodwill through such actions, and their service as liaisons for families has the potential to reduce family stress.

When notification of a student death is handled properly, family members will have a sense that their loved one mattered to the institution and can be left with a feeling of goodwill. Family members have regularly told me how much they appreciated the personal attention, kindness, and consideration surrounding their loved one's death that they received from professionals on my campus. A number of universities include information on risk management in the section of their Web site that addresses student deaths and the process of death notification (see, for example, the Web sites for Virginia Tech, http://www.vt.edu; American University, http://www.american.edu; and the University of Northern Iowa, http://www,uni.edu).

In the short term, families need an individual at the institution who will listen to them and spend as much time as needed to help them come to terms with the tragedy (Stone, 2007). My personal experience is that this is particularly helpful in dealing with families. When a tragic accident took the lives of two of our international students, one family came to the university for help. None of the family members had ever been in the United States, and they were unsure how to proceed with the most basic aspects surrounding how death is handled in this country. The associate dean of students and I met with the family. The associate dean went with the father to locate the student's bank and assist in closing accounts and negotiating legal and financial matters. I went with the mother and other family members to find and gain access to the student's apartment to pack the student's belongings.

In the long term, family members can be assisted by memorial services held either each semester or each year to which families and friends are invited. At Purdue, we hold a memorial service each spring and fall semester for students who have died during that time. It is called Golden Taps and was modeled after the Silver Taps held at Texas A&M. It is a nondenominational and simple ceremony, attended by family, friends, fellow students, and various campus professionals. Golden Taps is a collaborative event, with planning and participation by the Office of the Dean of Students, university residence halls, campus musical organizations, and Purdue student government. At this ceremony, family members are presented with a certificate of institutional attendance for the deceased.

NEW DIRECTIONS FOR STUDENT SERVICES • DOI: 10.1002/ss

Self-Care Recommendations for Campus Professionals with Death Notification Responsibilities

Campus professionals with death notification responsibilities are exposed to repeated stressful situations that can lead to burnout. Due to federal laws that protect the privacy of student education records and professional ethical guidelines, campus professionals are limited in discussing their experiences. Campus professionals need a good support system in their work environment. The psychological burden of death notification is another good argument for why staff should make death notification in pairs (Brooks and others, 1992). The two staff members in each team can (and should) take time to review each death notification experience shortly after the event.

Each death notification is unique in its details and the individuals who are involved. Campus professionals must be prepared to expect the unexpected. Because of the variety of ways that people respond, the notification team never knows what will happen. Going into situations that are so unpredictable makes it difficult to plan ahead or prepare. Sometimes the reactions are unsettlingly strong, and the professionals are not impervious to these emotions. Although staff members must stay calm and in control during notification, the fact is that they are participating in events that will change the lives of the people they are addressing. It is quite normal that these experiences affect the persons delivering the bad news.

Not only should the team review their experiences, but discussion should also take place with their supervisors. Other staff members can be of great assistance through expressing their appreciation for the difficult work done by the notification team. They can offer their support even in simple ways, such as asking if the staff are OK or thanking them for shouldering this emotionally trying and psychologically demanding responsibility. Policies such as allowing the team members to come in later in the day if they have worked late the night before engaged in a death notification or a class or group discussion or to leave early in the day if they have spent several hours with a bereaved student or family can help reduce burnout. Support staff can take responsibility for canceling and rescheduling the campus professionals' appointments and assisting the team in any other way that may be necessary.

Campus professionals responsible for death notification should take good physical and mental care of themselves. This recommendation may seem to be nothing more than common sense, but the cycle of the academic school year can overwhelm a campus professional before the person even realizes it is happening. A death loss may occur at a time of the year when staff are already overwhelmed by student orientation, Greek recruitment periods, finals, or other events that make it hard for staff to maintain a balance between work and their personal lives. It is particularly important during these "crunch" times that campus professionals find time to exercise, eat healthy, engage in hobbies and other activities, interact with family and friends, and attend to their spiritual needs. Individuals and teams must be aware of and attend to symptoms of stress such as difficulty falling asleep or waking early and being unable to go back to sleep, nightmares, loss of appetite or overeating, irritability, and feeling overwhelmed with work.

Campus professionals should use available resources such as consulting with a supervisor, using the Employee Assistance Program, and taking time between semesters to renew and refresh. Most of all, those who perform death notifications need to remember the importance and value of the service they provide. Although their work may not be glamorous or involve public praise or attention, the individuals they work with will remember them and be thankful for their compassion and professionalism years after the death notification interaction.

Conclusion

Working with students and families during one of their most difficult life events can be a rewarding experience. Notification of the death of a loved one is a moment in time that people are not likely to forget (Rando, 1988). My experience is that students and families appreciate how they are treated during this difficult time. Campus professionals must remember to take care in the details of how a student is notified. Following up with offers to talk and sending letters to faculty members will let the student know that you are sincere. Demonstrating to family members that their loved one was not just a number on your campus but a person who mattered to staff and friends will go a long way in determining how they remember the death and their feelings about the institution. And taking care of yourself so that you will be able to continue in this challenging role gives you the strength to handle the difficult task of death notification in a caring and professional manner.

References

Brooks, S., and others. "In Person, in Time: Recommended Procedures for Death Notification." [http://www.nationalcops.org/forms/in_person.pdf]. 1992.

Doka, K. J. Disenfranchised Grief: New Directions, Challenges, and Strategies for Practice. Champaign, Ill.: Research Press, 2002.

Goodrum, S. "The Interaction Between Thoughts and Emotions Following the News of a Loved One's Murder." Omega, 2005, 51, 143–160.

Iserson, K. V. Grave Words: Notifying Survivors About Sudden, Unexpected Deaths. Tucson, Ariz.: Galen Press, 1999.

Leash, R. M. Death Notification: A Practical Guide to the Process. Hinesburg, Vt.: Upper Access Books, 1994.

Lord, J. H. Trauma, Death, and Death Notification: A Seminar for Professional Counselors and Victim Advocates. Washington, D.C.: U.S. Department of Health and Human Services, 2000.

Rando, T. A. How to Go On Living When Someone You Love Dies. Lexington, Mass.: Lexington Books, 1988.

Servaty-Seib, H. L., and Hamilton, L. A. "Educational Performance and Persistence of Bereaved College Students." *Journal of College Student Development,* 2006, *47,* 225–233.

Stevenson, R. G. "The Role of the School." In K. J. Doka (ed.), *Children Mourning: Mourning Children.* Washington, D.C.: Hospice Foundation of America, 1995.

Stewart, A. E. "Complicated Bereavement and Posttraumatic Stress Disorder Following Fatal Car Crashes: Recommendations for Death Notification Practice." *Death Studies,* 1999, *23,* 289–321.

Stone, G. "Death Notification on Campus." Presentation at the symposium "Advocating for Bereaved College Students: Clinical and Systemic Strategies" (H. L. Servaty-Seib, chair.) at the annual convention of the American Psychological Association, San Francisco, Aug. 20, 2007.

LOU ANN HAMILTON is a clinical social worker and counselor in the Office of the Dean of Students at Purdue University.

NEW DIRECTIONS FOR STUDENT SERVICES • DOI: 10.1002/ss

8

When a student dies, administrators are confronted with a number of tasks and issues. This chapter provides practical guidance for responding to student death.

Student Death Protocols: A Practitioner's Perspective

Cheryl M. Callahan, Erin K. Fox

Student death on college campuses is a reality that occurs all too often, and dealing with the aftermath of a student's death is something that all higher education administrators must be prepared to address. Given the proliferation of media outlets, breaking news reports, and instant technologies used by students today, news about these deaths can spread quickly.

Regardless of whether the death is accidental, intentional, or violent, emotions run high for all persons involved with the victim as well as within the larger college community. Understanding the impact of these emotions is essential, and we must address the aftermath in both caring and rational ways. This chapter provides suggestions for practice in the case of a student's death as well as a rationale for preparing for such an event before it happens.

Preparation for the Aftermath of a Student Death

Because of the reality of death among college students, each institution must have at least a broad outline of steps to be taken in the immediate aftermath of a death. It is important that staff members from across the campus be aware of these steps, because information about a student death can come from any number of sources, including the media, the police, a parent, another student, or even a student from another institution.

Although every instance of student death is different, there are several steps administrators can take to prepare to respond to the death of a student

NEW DIRECTIONS FOR STUDENT SERVICES, no. 121, Spring 2008   © Wiley Periodicals, Inc.
Published online in Wiley InterScience (www.interscience.wiley.com) • DOI: 10.1002/ss.269

(or a group of students) (Crafts, 1985; Halberg, 1986; McCauley and Powell, 2007; Streufert, 2004).

Campus Coordination. Campus emergencies are just that and can occur at any time of the day or night. They do not occur at the convenience of staff and administrators, and campus professionals must stop whatever they are doing to address the situation at hand. Such is the case when a student dies. This could occur during the night or on weekends and holidays, so a communication plan is essential. Actions taken will depend on when and how the news is received.

Awareness of the larger campus community about its student death protocol will enable a more rapid response to the situation. To be prepared for such emergencies, campuses should designate a single office as the coordinator for all activities related to a student's death. Very often this is the office of the dean of students or the vice-president for student affairs. Identify one person in that office as the primary contact, with a second person designated as that person's backup. (For the purposes of this chapter, the primary contact is referred to as the campus coordinator.) Any office contacted regarding a student's death must get in touch with the campus coordinator as soon as possible. The campus coordinator must react quickly and sensitively to both the family and the larger college community. Appropriate protocols and procedures must be implemented with little notice, and communication with all affected by the death must be established almost immediately.

For example, if the campus coordinator is notified that a student has died in an off-campus fire in the early morning hours, he or she will want to establish communications with key members of the campus community before the media "hit the street" with the story. In particular, the coordinator will need to understand if communication has been established with the family by outside agencies such as the local police or fire department (which is more likely if the fire has occurred off campus) before he or she makes contact with that family. If the fire occurs on campus, the coordinator and members of the staff will likely be among the first on the scene, even if there are no fatalities.

To facilitate communication, the campus coordinator must have current contact information for all parties who need to be notified immediately and those who need to be accessible. This list of critical responders will be defined in the protocols already established and can include the president, university-media relations staff, counseling center staff or crisis team members, and legal counsel.

Determining who would notify the family of a student death (if it is not the campus coordinator) is the first step. This might be a police officer, a counseling center representative, or a campus minister on a religiously affiliated college campus. Having multiple individuals communicating with the family can create confusion at a very difficult time and can also increase the chance of miscommunication.

The coordinator might also be the point of contact for the media, although, depending on the circumstances surrounding the death, another staff member may assume this responsibility. The campus coordinator will need to gather important information regarding the deceased for reference in addressing both internal and external constituents, including other campus offices as well as media representatives. Information would include the student's full name and local address (either on or off campus), name and address of closest relatives (parents, guardians, spouse, and so on), date and cause of death, enrollment status and major (of more interest to campus offices), and how the college became aware of the death (of more interest to family and media). Use of common sense is critical in any conversations with media representatives as well as sensitivity to the needs and requests from the family regarding their privacy. Generally, the media will be much more interested if the death is the result of violence, alcohol, or hazing activities than if it resulted from an automobile accident or suicide (which should generate little or no media interest if the situation is handled appropriately by law enforcement officials—see Chapter Six).

Checklist of Activities. Develop a checklist of activities to be considered in the initial aftermath of a student's death. While some of these activities will apply to all situations, some may not apply if the deceased student lived off campus or was a non-traditional-age student. Taking cues from family members will assist in determining if all activities are appropriate or not. The checklist of activities could be as lengthy as an institution desires (a sample is presented in Exhibit 8.1) but should include at least the following for immediate attention (within twenty-four hours):

- Identification of those students who were closest to the deceased (for example, significant others, members of student organizations in which the deceased was active, residence hall friends and RAs, and so on). These groups will generally identify themselves quickly, either formally or informally.
- Activation of a crisis response team or counseling center staff (or both) to meet with affected student groups, faculty, and family members, as appropriate. Don't forget staff who may have been first responders or at the scene of the death. They may be the most affected but may have been trained not to show their emotions.
- A notification listing of all offices that maintain any form of student records: registrar, financial aid, student health, parking, career services, food services, housing, campus post office, student accounts, student conduct, library, legal counsel, and all relevant others.
- A notification listing of offices that need to remove the deceased's name from files or systems such as computing accounts, voice-mail systems, alumni affairs, academic departments (for example, the student's major), and so on.
- Formal sympathy notification to the family; this is often done by the college president, although sometimes by a designee.
- Contact information for helping family or students who wish to have a memorial service.

Exhibit 8.1. Sample Checklist

This checklist from the University of California–Berkeley incorporates many of the tasks appearing in various protocols and procedures regarding student death. It is the campus coordinator's final checklist, used to ensure that all tasks have been completed.

Coordinator's Final Checklist
Take a minute to check that you have completed all the necessary tasks.

Within the first 24 hours

__ Did you notify the Chancellor's Immediate Office and Housing, if applicable?
__ Did you communicate with the family and establish a relationship with a designated family member?
__ Did you complete the death report and email it to the following departments?
  __ Admissions and Enrollment
  __ ASUC
  __ Cal Parents
  __ Chancellor's Immediate Office
  __ Department (if appropriate)
  __ Employee Relations/HR
  __ Financial Aid
  __ Office of Student Life
  __ Payroll
  __ Public Affairs
  __ Registrar's Office
  __ Residential and Student Service Programs/Housing and Dining
  __ Risk Management
  __ Services for International Students and Scholars (SISS)
  __ UC Police
  __ UHS
__ Was the student an employee of the university? If so, contact department end employee in HRMS using TRM/DEA. Did you contact the HR Benefits Unit?
__ Did you check with the Registrar to verify if there are other students with the same name? Did you notify same-name students and parents?
__ Have you helped the family representative contact campus services such as UC Benefits, and communicated regarding personal belongings, financial obligations, and so on?
__ Have you called Counseling and Psychological Services for help in addressing the needs of students, faculty, staff and family?
__ Did you contact Student Activities and Services regarding student group affiliations?
__ Have you provided consultation on a memorial event to interested departments/organizations? Have you consulted with the family representative about private memorial events? Have you communicated this information, along with dates and times, to the relevant campus community?
__ Have you informed family and other interested parties about the Virtual Memorial?

During 24 to 48 hours

__ Did you review info on Benefits and Payroll, if applicable, in order to discuss with the family of the deceased?
__ The Registrar's Office will coordinate refunds from the following:
  __ Cashier's Office
  __ CARS Billing
  __ Intercollegiate Athletics and Recreational Sports
  __ Library

___ Loans and Receivables
___ Parking and Transportation
___ Summer Session
___ The Registrar's Office will also notify the following:
   ___ Alumni Records
   ___ California Alumni Association
   ___ Cal Monthly
   ___ College Advisor
   ___ Department Chair
   ___ Instructors
   ___ OP Student Academic Services
   ___ OP Education Testing Services, and Application Processing
___ Have you worked with the Vice Chancellor of Undergraduate Affairs to coordinate condolences? Have you identified the campus representative to attend any on- or off-campus memorial events?
___ If applicable, did you consult with Public Affairs and the Registrar on the appropriate release of information?

48+ hours

___ Have you reviewed the following issues for applicability?
   ___ Death certificates
   ___ Donations and gifts
   ___ Family of deceased and travel expenses
   ___ Cause of Death education
   ___ Multiple deaths
   ___ Obituary
   ___ Posthumous awards
   ___ Transportation of remains
___ Have you inventoried personal and professional possessions and arranged for retrieval?

Source: University of California–Berkeley. "Guidelines for Responding to Death: Coordinator's Final Checklist." Copyright © 2002 by the Regents of the University of California. Reprinted with permission.

- Determination of how or if the whole campus community will be informed of the death via a mass e-mail, campus newspaper posting, and so on.
- Determination if external audiences need to be notified (for example, the board of trustees) based on the circumstances of the student's death.

Additional activities to consider within the first twenty-four to forty-eight hours include the following:

- Establish communication between those interested in a memorial service (could be family or students or both) and campus ministers.
- Coordinate the family's arrival to the campus (if applicable) and provide lodging and transportation (if possible and needed).
- Determine who will attend the funeral as representatives from the institution.

- Consider initial arrangements for packing the deceased's belongings for return to the family.
- Facilitate the establishment of a memorial fund or other contributions through conversations with the family if requested. In some situations involving multiple students (such as a residence hall or apartment fire), community members beyond the campus may make inquiries about how and where to make donations to support others who survived but were affected by the incident.

The following activities may be done beyond the first few days (document all that you can):

- Returning the student's belongings to the family.
- Ensuring that refunds of tuition and fees have been made and that the appropriate withdrawal documents have been completed.
- Facilitating reimbursement of financial aid, loan cancellation, and similar matters.
- Continued monitoring of those affected by the death and provision of support services for students or faculty and staff members (or both), as appropriate.

Crisis Response Team. Since the events of September 11, 2001, many institutions have formed crisis response teams. These teams are designed to move into a situation where emotions run high. They can be as small or as large as the institution deems necessary. Their roles may differ from one event to another, but their existence can be a comforting support system for the first responders to a student death and for the campus coordinator.

Members of a crisis response team can come from many sectors of the campus community and can provide a great opportunity for interdepartmental as well as intradepartmental collaboration (Duncan and Miser, 2000; McCauley and Powell, 2007). Potential members include campus ministers; counseling center staff; faculty from disciplines such as psychology, counseling, or religion; student affairs staff trained in crisis management; and other administrators and faculty who simply care about students. A leader must be designated and is often the counseling center director or the dean of students. Regular communication between and among team members is also important so that everyone knows each other's strengths and will know how to support each other in a crisis as well as support those most affected by the given situation.

It is most important for everyone involved in responding to a student death or other crisis to understand the role that this team can play. Be it simply standing by at a memorial service to reach out to those who are emotionally distraught to sitting with a small group to support the grieving process, team members can supply the much needed additional time and energy that the campus coordinator simply does not have.

Policies and Protocols

For many administrators and college student affairs professionals, it is difficult to think about developing policies and protocols for student deaths (as well as other campus crises). Most want to believe that their training has prepared them to deal with each situation in a unique and appropriate manner. Although their training may have prepared them to deal with crises, it is in times of crisis that they often forget to do that one thing that would have made the response better and stronger because they, too, can get caught up in the emotion of the moment.

Student death protocols are plentiful. A simple Internet search turns up many examples of how campus colleagues around the country are preparing for such an eventuality. Many of them include ideas and checklists similar to the information in this chapter. Some are very short; others are lengthy and quite detailed. The important thing to keep in mind is that each institution needs to consider its own culture and its own organization and to develop a protocol that is appropriate for its community. While there are certainly commonalities among protocols, there also are significant differences. A list of some sample protocols can be found in Exhibit 8.2.

There are also other policies on every campus that will come into play at the time of a student's death. Recognizing and understanding how they will be implemented at the time of a student death is important. They might include withdrawal policies, refund policies (related to tuition and fees, parking fees, and so on), student account policies (for example, unpaid student health fees and overdue library books), and academic policies (does the family receive a posthumous honorary degree?). It is important that all policies be reviewed to know which will need to be considered at the time of a student death and how a modification of the policy might be considered at such a time. A grieving family should not have to contend with bureaucratic red tape.

One policy that may not exist speaks directly to how the institution will handle information that was protected by the Family Educational Rights and Privacy Act (FERPA) prior to the student's death. This law no longer applies to a deceased student, so it is important that each institution consider developing its own policy to address what information will be shared and with whom.

Campus Crisis Communication Plan

Crisis communication plans are not new to higher education. They have existed for a long time and address any number of crises, including an on-campus fire; a hazing event; a natural disaster such as a hurricane, tornado, or winter storm; or a public health issue such as an outbreak of meningitis or measles. The ability to communicate with one another and external constituent groups in a timely manner is important. It is likely at the time of a

Exhibit 8.2. Sample Protocols and Procedures

The following institutions have formulated protocols and procedures that can be consulted online for review. They vary in content and format because they are developed to suit the unique context of the individual institution, as all policies should be.

Fordham University:
http://www.fordham.edu/images/safety/emergency%20management%20plan.pdf
Frostburg State University:
http://www.frostburg.edu/admin/policies/crisismanagementplan.pdf
Glendale Community College:
http://www.gc.maricopa.edu/facultystaffhandbook/index.cfm?id=1253
Ohio University:
http://www.ohiou.edu/policy2/20-001.html
Oregon State University:
http://oregonstate.edu/deanofstudents/cirt.html
Pennsylvania State University:
http://www.sa.psu.edu/death_response/sd_admin.html
Queen's University, Belfast:
http://www.qub.ac.uk/directorates/AcademicStudentAffairs/FileStore/Filetoupload,
53812,en.pdf
University of California–Berkeley:
http://death-response.chance.berkeley.edu/undergraduate/index.html
University of California–Los Angeles:
http://www.adminvc.ucla.edu/appm/entry_policies.asp?vSection=public/160-2.htm
University of Edinburgh:
http://www.registry.ed.ac.uk/Student/Emergency_Situations.htm
University of Wisconsin–Eau Claire:
http://www.uwec.edu/sdd/emergencies.htm
University of Wisconsin–Whitewater:
http://www.uww.edu/uwwhdbk/policies/StudentDeathProcedures.htm

Note: All institutions listed here have granted us permission to include them in this listing. The URLs are current at the time of this printing; a simple Internet search on some of the keywords in these URLs will yield additional examples.

student death that such a plan might be enacted, although the extent to which that plan will be carried out will depend on the cause and location of death.

Important considerations in this communication plan at the time of a student death include the following:

- Who needs to be informed about the student's death, and how quickly must this be done?
- Who is the campus spokesperson for the media and the external community (if needed)?
- Who will develop public statements? Will they need to be reviewed by legal counsel or others beforehand?
- Who will communicate accurate and timely information to the internal campus community?

Summary

Student death is a situation no one wants to face, but it is a reality that is likely to arise during every student affairs professional's career. Much can be learned from others who have faced similar challenges, and this area is no exception. The suggestions in this chapter are intended to get the ball rolling on campuses that do not yet have protocols and policies in place. What is most important for all student affairs practitioners is to share lessons and practices so that others can benefit from them. Although each campus has a unique culture and ways of dealing with tragedy, others can adapt ideas to improve their way of doing business. Therefore, you must continue to share effective practices at professional conferences, continue to support your colleagues when you learn of a tragedy on their campus, and make yourself available to provide solace and encouragement and to reassure those who have been affected by the tragedy that you care. We are all in this together.

References

Crafts, R. "Student Affairs Response to Student Death." In E. S. Zinner (ed.), *Coping with Death on Campus.* New Directions for Student Services, no. 31. San Francisco: Jossey-Bass, 1985.

Duncan, M. A., and Miser, K. M. "Dealing with Campus Crisis." In M. J. Barr and M. K. Desler (eds.), *The Handbook of Student Affairs Administration.* San Francisco: Jossey-Bass, 2000.

Halberg, L. J. "Death of a College Student: Response by Student Services Professionals on One Campus." *Journal of Counseling and Development,* 1986, *64,* 411–412.

McCauley, R. F., and Powell, J. D. "Campus Response Teams: The Need for Coordination." In R. Cintron, E. T. Weathers, and K. Garlough (eds.), *College Student Death: Guidance for a Caring Campus.* Lanham, Md.: University Press of America, 2007.

Streufert, B. J. "Death on Campuses: Common Postvention Strategies in Higher Education." *Death Studies,* 2004, *28,* 151–172.

CHERYL (CHERRY) M. CALLAHAN *is associate vice-chancellor for student affairs at the University of North Carolina at Greensboro and a past president of the National Association of Student Personnel Administrators (NASPA).*

ERIN K. FOX *is the director of first-year programs at Saint Andrews Presbyterian College in Laurinburg, North Carolina.*

INDEX

Adams, N., 23
Adams, V., 57, 58
African American students, 35–36
American College Health Association National College Health Assessment, 21
American Psychiatric Association, 48
AMF (National Students of Ailing Mothers and Fathers) Support Network, 11, 58–59
Anderson, A., 17, 18, 20, 33
Anderson, R. N., 1
Anger reaction, 63–64
Association for Death Education Counseling, 43
Attachment theory, 8
Attig, T., 8, 9, 34, 46, 47, 48, 49, 53

Baldwin, S. A., 20, 34
Balk, D. E., 1, 5, 6, 7, 8, 9, 10, 12, 14, 16, 18, 21, 22, 28, 30, 41, 43, 47, 53
Ball State University, 81
Banning, J. H., 15, 20
Bates, C., 64, 66, 73
Baxter Magolda, M. B., 15, 19
Becker, K., 23
Behavioral effects of bereavement, 9
Belenky, M. F., 15, 19
Benefit-finding adaptation, 33–34
Bereavement: clinical interventions/other responses to, 9–10; effects of, 8–9, 29–30; expectations by peers regarding, 53; finding meaning following loss, 30–36; institution policies/protocols on, 23; practical points to remember and apply about, 36–37. *See also* Grief; Grieving students
Bereavement research: on coping strategies, 18; diversity factor of, 35–36, 37; on grief responses, 29–30; recommendations on institutional, 10
Bereavement theories: college ecology, 20–21; developmental, 15–20
Bereavement training. *See* Grief education
Berg, D. H., 48
Berson, R. J., 10
Binge drinkers, 21
Blackboard, 59
Blimbling, G., 51

Bonanno, G. A., 28, 29, 48, 52
Bowlby, J., 8
Bowman, R. L., 57, 58
Bowman, V. E., 57
Branson, M. L., 65, 73
Braun, M. J., 48
Brillant, J. J., 57, 58
Brooks, S., 78, 79, 81, 84
Brooks-Harris, J. E., 57
Bryant, R. A., 66, 67, 68, 73
Burleson, B. R., 54

Calhoun, L., 31
Callahan, C. M., 2, 69, 73, 87, 95
Campbell, F. R., 72
Campus: bereavement centers in, 10–11, 22–23; CDC guidelines for suicide applied to, 70–71; coordinating emergency of student death on, 88–89; crisis communication plan for, 93–94; crisis response team on, 92; DRTs (death response teams) used on, 72; theories of campus ecology on environment of, 20–21. *See also* Institutions
Cardozo, P. J., 56, 57, 58
Cataldie, L., 72
Catlin, G., 16
CebCT, 59
Celotta, B., 67, 68, 69
Centers for Disease Control and Prevention (CDC), 70
Cepani, A., 66
Chesson, B. C., 11
Chickering, A. W., 15, 16, 17, 18, 23, 29
City University of New York (Brooklyn College), 6
Clark, C. A., 22, 43, 46
Clark, S., 63
Clinchy, B. M., 15, 19
Cognitive effects of bereavement, 9
Cognitive-structured developmental theories, 18–20
Coleman, R., 31
Colletti-Wetzel, J., 0, 9, 41, 43
Communication: acknowledging death loss, 54; campus coordination following student death, 88–89; taking the time to listen, 54; validating person-centeredness, 54–55

OTHER TITLES AVAILABLE IN THE
New Directions for Student Services Series
JOHN H. SCHUH, EDITOR-IN-CHIEF
ELIZABETH J. WHITT, ASSOCIATE EDITOR

SS120 **Responding to the Realities of Race on Campus**
Shaun R. Harper, Lori D. Patton
This volume of *New Directions for Student Services* illuminates several
realities regarding racism, cross-racial interaction, race-based educational
inequities, and campus racial climates in higher education. Authors describe
how student learning and development are stifled by the mistreatment of
race as a taboo topic on most college and university campuses. They also
discuss the disconnection between espoused and enacted institutional
values concerning inclusiveness and racial equity, as well as the need for
increased accountability and intentionality. In addition to igniting critical
consciousness about one of the most vexing problems in American higher
education, the chapters in this volume include several practical implications
for reducing racial toxins in campus environments and engaging students in
meaningful learning experiences about race inside and outside the
classroom.
ISBN: 978-04702-62030

SS119 **e-Portfolios: Emerging Opportunities for Student Affairs**
Jeff W. Garis, Jon C. Dalton
E-portfolios are increasingly important in higher education, both in the U.S.
and around the world. They are being designed and used to support the
learning process through reflection, in assessment-based systems that
support institutional accreditation, and in so-called showcase e-portfolios
that support students' career development and employment. This issue
presents the range of current systems, examines various design considerations associated with them, provides examples of models in place at selected
institutions, and stresses the importance for student affairs leadership of
creating a college- or university-wide e-portfolio delivery system.
ISBN: 978-04702-55216

SS118 **Key Issues in New Student Enrollment**
Thomas Crady, James Sumner
As the first decade of the twenty-first century draws to a close and the baby
boomlet ends, America's 4,000-odd colleges and universities will once again
be forced to deal with a declining number of secondary-school graduates.
Some institutions will become smaller, some will close, new student markets
will develop, and students who might have selected college X in the past will
select college Y instead. This volume brings into focus many of the key
issues American institutions of higher education will face in the next decade
as they encounter demographic changes much like those they confronted
when the baby boom ended in the 1980s. Will private industries continue
to try to reap financial benefits from the desire of both families and
institutions for status? Is the notion of meeting the full demonstrated
financial need of most admitted students gone forever? Is need-blind
admission at independent colleges a thing of the past? Will the marketplace
value of the SAT and ACT continue to slip? Will the goal of creating a
diverse student body run into further legal challenges and roadblocks? These

and other contemporary issues in new student enrollment are explored by a group of leading professionals who thoughtfully explore topics of special and passionate interest to them and to everyone, teachers and administrators alike, in America's colleges and universities.
ISBN: 978-04702-26209

SS117   **Student Affairs Staff as Teachers**
Emily L. Moore
The teaching role of student affairs professionals is gaining importance as colleges and universities emphasize retention and graduation of under-graduates. Student affairs professionals play a crucial role in the teaching-learning process. This issue of *New Directions for Student Services* explores the paradigm shift of student affairs staff from enablers to teachers. It addresses this phenomenon, beginning with a framing chapter on the act and art of teaching and extending through the first days of the first year, the first-year experience, learning communities, and the seamless web of student and academic affairs that has formed in a small college. The volume concludes with a futuristic examination of the expanding roles and responsibilities of student affairs professionals.
ISBN: 978-07879-9722-9

SS116   **The Small College Dean**
Sarah B. Westfall
Senior student affairs professionals in small colleges have their own challenges and rewards that are often overlooked by the literature. This volume's authors give insight to working at colleges with fewer than 5,000 students, with chapters about the dean's portfolio, recruiting and retaining staff, academic vs. student affairs, the vice president's role, and more. This volume is a primer on serving as a dean at a small college.
ISBN: 0-7879-9580-0

SS115   **Supporting Graduate and Professional Students**
Melanie J. Guentzel, Becki Elkins Nesheim
Student affairs practice has historically focused on undergraduates and left support (academic, social, professional) for graduate students to their respective department or college. But academic departments emphasize cognitive development of a scholar rather than the psychosocial aspects of the graduate student experience. This volume focuses on the needs of graduate and professional students that can be addressed specifically by student affairs professionals.
ISBN: 0-7879-9057-4

SS114   **Understanding Students in Transition: Trends and Issues**
Frankie Santos Laanan
This volume is designed for practitioners (in student services, teaching, or administration) seeking to understand the changing realities of today's diverse, complex college students. It includes recommendations for research, practice, and policy. The research and practical examples can be applied to multiple student populations: recent high school graduates, community college transfers, and older adults returning to education.
ISBN: 0-7879-8679-8

SS113   **Gambling on Campus**
George S. McClellan, Thomas W. Hardy, Jim Caswell
Gambling has become a serious concern on college campuses, fueled by the surge of online gaming and the national poker craze, and is no longer a fringe activity. This informative issue includes perspectives from students, suggestions for research, frameworks for campus policy development, and

case studies of education and intervention. Anyone interested in supporting student success must be informed about gambling on campus.
ISBN: 0-7879-8597-X

SS112   **Technology in Student Affairs: Supporting Student Learning and Services**
Kevin Kruger
Information technology has helped create a 24/7 self-service way for students to interact with campus administrative functions, whether they're on campus or distance learners. And new technologies could move beyond administrative into student learning and development. This volume is not a review of current technology in student affairs. Rather, it focuses on how technology is changing the organization of student affairs, how to use it effectively, and how lines are blurring between campus-based and distance learning.
ISBN: 0-7879-8362-4

SS111   **Gender Identity and Sexual Orientation: Research, Policy, and Personal Perspectives**
Ronni L. Sanlo
Lesbian, gay, bisexual, and transgender people have experienced homophobia, discrimination, exclusion, and marginalization in the academy, from subtle to overt. Yet LGBT people have been a vital part of the history of American higher education. This volume describes current issues, research, and policies, and it offers ways for institutions to support and foster the success of LGBT students, faculty, and staff.
ISBN: 0-7879-8328-4

SS110   **Developing Social Justice Allies**
Robert D. Reason, Ellen M. Broido, Tracy L. Davis, Nancy J. Evans
Social justice allies are individuals from dominant groups (for example, whites, heterosexuals, men) who work to end the oppression of target group members (people of color, homosexuals, women). Student affairs professionals have a history of philosophical commitment to social justice, and this volume strives to provide the theoretical foundation and practical strategies to encourage the development of social justice and civil rights allies among students and colleagues.
ISBN: 0-7879-8077-3

SS109   **Serving Native American Students**
Mary Jo Tippeconnic Fox, Shelly C. Lowe, George S. McClellan
The increasing Native American enrollment on campuses nationwide is something to celebrate; however, the retention rate for Native American students is the lowest in higher education, a point of tremendous concern. This volume's authors—most of them Native American—address topics such as enrollment trends, campus experiences, cultural traditions, student services, ignorance about Indian country issues, expectations of tribal leaders and parents, and other challenges and opportunities encountered by Native students.
ISBN: 0-7879-7971-6

SS108   **Using Entertainment Media in Student Affairs Teaching and Practice**
Deanna S. Forney, Tony W. Cawthon
Reaching all students may require going beyond traditional methods, especially in the out-of-classroom environments typical to student affairs. Using films, music, television shows, and popular books can help students learn. This volume—good for both practitioners and educators—shares effective approaches to using entertainment media to facilitate understanding of general student development, multiculturalism, sexual orientation, gender issues, leadership, counseling, and more.
ISBN: 0-7879-7926-0

SS107   Developing Effective Programs and Services for College Men
         Gar E. Kellom
         This volume's aim is to better understand the challenges facing college men,
         particularly at-risk men. Topics include enrollment, retention, academic
         performance, women's college perspectives, men's studies perspectives,
         men's health issues, emotional development, and spirituality. Chapters
         deliver recommendations and examples about programs and services that
         improve college men's learning experiences and race, class, and gender
         awareness.
         ISBN: 0-7879-7772-1

SS106   Serving the Millennial Generation
         Michael D. Coomes, Robert DeBard
         Focuses on the next enrollment boom, students born after 1981, known as
         the Millennial generation. Examines these students' attitudes, beliefs, and
         behaviors, and makes recommendations to student affairs practitioners for
         working with them. Discusses historical and cultural influences that shape
         generations, demographics, teaching and learning patterns of Millennials,
         and how student affairs can best educate and serve them.
         ISBN: 0-7879-7606-7

SS105   Addressing the Unique Needs of Latino American Students
         Anna M. Ortiz
         Explores the experiences of the fast-growing population of Latinos in higher
         education, and what these students need from student affairs. This volume
         examines the influence of the Latino family, socioeconomic levels, cultural
         barriers, and other factors to understand the challenges faced by Latinos.
         Discusses administration, student groups, community colleges, support
         programs, cultural identity, Hispanic-Serving Institutions, and more.
         ISBN: 0-7879-7479-X

SS104   Meeting the Needs of African American Women
         Mary F. Howard-Hamilton
         Identifies and explores the critical needs for African American women as
         students, faculty, and administrators. This volume introduces theoretical
         frameworks and practical applications for addressing challenges; discusses
         identity and spirituality; explores the importance of programming support in
         recruitment and retention; describes the benefits of mentoring; and provides
         illuminating case studies of black women's issues in higher education.
         ISBN: 0-7879-7280-0

SS103   Contemporary Financial Issues in Student Affairs
         John H. Schuh
         This volume addresses the challenging financial situation facing higher
         education and offers creative solutions for student affairs staff. Topics
         include the differences between public and private institutions in funding
         student activities, how to demonstrate financial accountability to
         stakeholders, plus ways to address budget challenges in student unions,
         health centers, campus recreation, counseling centers, and student housing.
         ISBN: 0-7879-7173-1

NEW DIRECTIONS FOR STUDENT SERVICES
Order Form
SUBSCRIPTIONS AND SINGLE ISSUES

DISCOUNTED BACK ISSUES:

Use this form to receive **20% off** all back issues of New Directions for Student Services. All single issues priced at **$22.40** (normally $28.00)

TITLE   ISSUE NO.   ISBN

_____   _____   _____

_____   _____   _____

_____   _____   _____

Call 888-378-2537 or see mailing instructions below. When calling, mention the promotional code, JB7ND, to receive your discount.

SUBSCRIPTIONS: *(1 year, 4 issues)*

☐ New Order   ☐ Renewal

U.S.	☐ Individual: $80	☐ Institutional: $195
Canada/Mexico	☐ Individual: $80	☐ Institutional: $235
All Others	☐ Individual: $104	☐ Institutional: $269

Call 888-378-2537 or see mailing and pricing instructions below. Online subscriptions are available at www.interscience.wiley.com.

Copy or detach page and send to:

John Wiley & Sons, Journals Dept, 5th Floor
989 Market Street, San Francisco, CA 94103-1741

Order Form can also be faxed to: 888-481-2665

Issue/Subscription Amount: $ _____	**SHIPPING CHARGES:**	
Shipping Amount: $ _____	SURFACE	Domestic Canadian
(for single issues only—subscription prices include shipping)	First Item	$5.00 $6.00
Total Amount: $ _____	Each Add'l Item	$3.00 $1.50

(No sales tax for U.S. subscriptions. Canadian residents, add GST for subscription orders. Individual rate subscriptions must be paid by personal check or credit card. Individual rate subscriptions may not be resold as library copies.)

☐ Payment enclosed (U.S. check or money order only. All payments must be in U.S. dollars.)

☐ VISA ☐ MC ☐ Amex # _____ Exp. Date_____

Card Holder Name _____ Card Issue # _____

Signature_____ Day Phone _____

☐ Bill Me (U.S. institutional orders only. Purchase order required.)

Purchase order # _____
　　　　　　　　　　Federal Tax ID13559302   GST 89102 8052

Name_____

Address _____

Phone _____ E-mail _____

JB7ND

NEW DIRECTIONS FOR STUDENT SERVICES IS NOW AVAILABLE ONLINE AT WILEY INTERSCIENCE

What is Wiley InterScience?

Wiley InterScience is the dynamic online content service from John Wiley & Sons delivering the full text of over 300 leading scientific, technical, medical, and professional journals, plus major reference works, the acclaimed *Current Protocols* laboratory manuals, and even the full text of select Wiley print books online.

What are some special features of Wiley InterScience?

Wiley InterScience Alerts is a service that delivers table of contents via e-mail for any journal available on Wiley InterScience as soon as a new issue is published online.
Early View is Wiley's exclusive service presenting individual articles online as soon as they are ready, even before the release of the compiled print issue. These articles are complete, peer-reviewed, and citable.
CrossRef is the innovative multi-publisher reference linking system enabling readers to move seamlessly from a reference in a journal article to the cited publication, typically located on a different server and published by a different publisher.

How can I access Wiley InterScience?

Visit http://www.interscience.wiley.com

Guest Users can browse Wiley InterScience for unrestricted access to journal Tables of Contents and Article Abstracts, or use the powerful search engine.
Registered Users are provided with a *Personal Home Page* to store and manage customized alerts, searches, and links to favorite journals and articles. Additionally, Registered Users can view free Online Sample Issues and preview selected material from major reference works.
Licensed Customers are entitled to access full-text journal articles in PDF, with select journals also offering full-text HTML.

How do I become an Authorized User?

Authorized Users are individuals authorized by a paying Customer to have access to the journals in Wiley InterScience. For example, a university that subscribes to Wiley journals is considered to be the Customer. Faculty, staff and students authorized by the university to have access to those journals in Wiley InterScience are Authorized Users. Users should contact their Library for information on which Wiley journals they have access to in Wiley InterScience.